KESTREL KLEE

By the same author

THE HERON GARTH
KRARK, The Story of a Carrion Crow

KESTREL KLEE

Kenneth Richmond

BARRY SHURLOCK

BARRY SHURLOCK
& Co. (Publishers) Ltd
22 Gayhurst Close
Reading RG4 0QW

New Impression 1973

ISBN 0 903330 05 9

Printed in Great Britain by
Redwood Press Ltd
Trowbridge, Wiltshire

KESTREL KLEE

I

THIS is a tale of Klee, Winnower of Winds, the sky-rider. A tale, not the life-story, for of that no one will ever know much: it has long disappeared into nothingness, leaving no trace in its passing, like the softest stroke of plume on air. None can know, let alone record its intimate realities, —not even the clear wild brain of Klee himself.

A hawk knows nothing of memory. His life has neither before nor after, only the swift fierceness of a perpetual moment. A life of sensation rather than of thought; it is like the pages of a book turning, skimming, turning, skimming, and each leaf with its sharp pictures irretrievably shutting behind the eye for ever. Perhaps at times, dozing or preening after his bath, some dim recollection of his past life may have wavered across Klee's mind; but only for a moment. Awake, his mind was no more than a blaze of light, a bright image of alternate earth and clouds, clearer than finest glass, held in the circles of his great, yellow-skinned eyes. Every detail was pin-sharp in that intense, unremitting focus,—the starry pimpernel blooms straggling beneath the wheat stems, the snail-shells by yon yellow stone (emptied yesterday by Spek the Song Thrush), the darker earth on the side of the great earth pile which showed that Sturr, the old mole, had this morning returned to his autumn seam (a point to remember),—these and a myriad other details filled and flooded his daily consciousness. Miraculous eye!—in it Klee had the greater part of his being. Asleep, he relapsed into a dreamless darkness.

His appearance? An aristocrat in every feather, Klee was more slender than sturdy, lithe and light-limbed. His broad wings (golden-chestnut, spotted and tipped with black) ended in long and knife-like pinions, and his cloud-grey tail opened and shut like a fan, answering each twist and sway of the wind. He was, in short, cut neatly,—a blend of delicacy and strength. A prince. In storms he had to nurse his motions to the gale's fury: he could not, like Hek the mad falcon, hurl himself into it like a steel bullet. Yet he could rocket earthwards just as dizzily as Hek at his maddest and pull out of the steepest dive far more quickly and gracefully. The slightest miscalculation as he swept down to land, leaf-light,—a fraction's error and the yellow, scaly shanks of his leg-bones would have snapped like match-sticks,—they were so thin. Yet whenever he clenched his black, sickled foot it was with a concentrated viciousness that was almost fanatical—as if a man were crushing stones between his bare fingers. His whole structure was compact of air and iron. His face was covered with tiniest feathers, softer than down, set off by a slashing black moustache, but from it there curved a great steel riving hook of a bill.

Such, in appearance, was Klee.

2

HE entered the world, spitting and snarling, in a May noon, hacking his way through the red-speckled shell until the white brilliance of the dazzling world burst open all round, tugging at his eyes until they hurt. All that day he lay cowering in the eyrie, too exhausted to raise his head or flick his lidless eyes, while the yellow egg-slime dried in clots upon his bedraggled down. He was a helpless little lump, a ball of white fluff, not two inches from top to bottom; all scrag and belly with two feet that clutched convulsively at the dead sticks with which the bottom of the nest was lined. He was the last and smallest of four. From the start he hated everything, his three sisters most of all. They were for ever squirming and twitching on top of him, pushing and crowding him out when the mother bird came to drop gobbets and slivers of raw, wet meat into their clamouring gullets. However hard he clawed and struggled, little Klee was always last served: so much so that in the end he drooped and grew almost lifeless for want of regular sustenance. Then a sort of blind fury would galvanize him into action, and as soon as he heard the first whuff of her returning wings he would urge himself towards the edge and thrust up his skinny throat, quivering and gaping to be fed. And she, knowing the signs (for Klee's mother was an old hand at the game—her sixth brood this, and she with the small-shot of half a dozen keepers embedded in her body), took care to see that from then on he received special attention.

Gradually he revived. In a fortnight he had sprouted his first waxy feathers. By this time the eyrie was becoming more and more unbearable. How he detested it!

There were bits of blackening bones, fur with the blood dried hard upon it,—they irritated his sensitive, scurfy skin and, however much he shifted, they rubbed and chafed him. There were flies settling around him all the time, buzzing and darting. He made petulant jabs at them with his head, but they always evaded him,—with a laconic insolence, settling almost at once only a few inches away: in the end he grew desperate and bit the nearest of his three sisters on the leg in sheer spite. In the scuffle that followed he got the worst of it, of course, but that was the affair of a moment: soon all four relapsed into forgetful passivity again. Their new feathers were giving all the young birds quite a lot of trouble. They felt ill at ease, heavy, without energy, and now when the parents returned the three sisters would often just lie inert, not even opening their maws to take the food that was still so liberally proffered them. Even Klee's appetite suffered, though he took advantage of the respite to catch up a little with the others in weight and size.

It was so hot! so oppressive! Most of the time he just lay there with his head hanging over the edge, his beak open and panting, as he glared at the pitiless arc of the sun. Usually when it grew quite unbearable the mother hawk came and stood over them, shielding and sheltering all four as best she could under her splayed wings. It was the same when it rained. Little Klee was always the first to shuffle underneath, snuggling into the softness of her body for protection.

At night she continued to brood them as jealously as if they were still eggs about to hatch, as jealously as she had done in their first days when they were naked, frog-like mites; and for all her outward fierceness she mothered them as tenderly as any nightingale, pulling them towards her, nuzzling them together with the smooth edge of her beak until all four were comfortably arranged, before she settled on them for the night. Klee never once needed persuasion in this,—he loved it almost as much as being fed. But the two oldest fledglings were always rather more unruly: they liked to be independent,—forage abroad on their own accounts,—to such an extent that they had to be dealt with quite roughly at times.

At the end of a month these two forward fledglings had grown even more venturesome. Every morning they would clamber out from the eyrie and sun themselves on the end branches of the great oak, blinking and occasionally waving their wings in a rather half-hearted fashion, and always looking most pleased with themselves. True, there was more room in the nest when they were gone: all the same, Klee envied them and would have followed if only he had dared. Out there the shadow of the leaves looked cool, and how fine it must be to sit in triumph on the bare bough with the whole world of greenery beneath! By this time, however, he had gained a pretty good idea of his immediate corner of the world: he had seen the rocks below, the dead acorns that exploded in the heat and fell with a crackle, bouncing from branch to branch, the dark drop,—and he was scared. He preferred to spend his time snatching at flies in the nest, exercising his sprouting limbs in safety.

Then one day the morning sun seemed suddenly to disappear. Klee felt a great weight behind his eyes and the blood tingling along his spine and the purple darkness closing in around him. The air was thick, very still: he wondered uneasily how long it would be before his mother returned. Now that they were all able to feed themselves, her visits had become much more intermittent than at first. Sometimes she would be away for hours, and then when she did come it was only to drop a mouse or a bleeding vole into the nest and away again. Klee had never seen much of his father: he knew him best by the nervous whinnying whistle he used to give whenever he brought food for the family; but now even that was a thing of the past.

It grew darker. The afternoon had become livid, menacing. Out on the branches the venturesome pair now sat glumly, limp, their heads sunk on their breasts.

Without prelude there was a blue flash, and a handful of stony hail was flung at Klee's head. Next moment great balls of white were bouncing all round him, stinging, stunning,—stoning him unmercifully. He cowered in among the sticks for protection, but it was battering at him ceaselessly, beating the life out of him until he squeaked in pain and panic, but still the blows kept on, harder, harder, heavier . . . In utter desperation he tried to urge himself towards the edge, heaving and scrabbling with his stumps of wings,—anywhere to escape that overhead terror. Another moment and he would have been over, but before he could reach it there was a rush of wings behind him. Wild-eyed, Klee's mother bundled him back under her tense wing, and reaching forward, nipped the nearest of his sisters by the scruff and pulled her back into the safety of the eyrie. The other two she could not reach; nor could she dare to go to their assistance. She stood there, straddled with distress, staring frantically.

Kikik . . . kikikikikik! she cried, torn with helpless anxiety.

But there was no answer. Her mate, riding and swinging in the clear sky far above the thunder shower, heard her cry without heeding: he thought she was angry. He had always been nervous of her sudden unaccountable moods, nervous of approaching the eyrie,—for since the young appeared she had always made it clear that the nest was *hers*, no place for him. Besides, he had lost interest in his family. With an idle shifting of his two outer tail feathers he merely took the freshening wind and glided comfortably off.

The squall's viciousness spent itself in five minutes. It just stopped. Instead, a fine soft rain came quietly down.

When at last he ventured to peep, Klee saw that the white layer with which the nest had been plastered was already slithering into water, the clots of hail thinning and melting, the wet black sticks beginning to show through again. He could feel it running and dripping down his mother's draggled breast, but when he tried to poke out she thrust him in again almost distractedly.

Kikikit! she called again, in sharp distress.

Next she stood up, shook herself,—a spray of drops,—and flew across to the branch where the two fledglings had had their stand. It was too late. One had already fallen and disappeared: the other lay beaten lifeless, caught in a cleft. She gave them not another thought, did not so much as touch either of them; in a moment she was back at the nest to tend the two survivors of this unexpected tragedy. Oh! she fussed them as never before, and Klee, more dead than alive, was glad of all her attentions, for in his reeling brain there was no spirit left, only a craving for comfort.

Oddly enough, his very backwardness served him in good stead after all. His unreadiness for exploration had been the only means of saving him from complete disaster. Even his one remaining sister had fared far worse. Unable to shuffle back in time, she had been exposed,—until her mother rescued her,—to the full blast of the storm: and the arrowy ice had smashed one eyeball to a dark wet hole. What had been a limpid iris, a circle of brightness, was now no more than a smeared mess dribbling down her wet cheeks, scarcely distinguishable from rain-water.

Klee knew her later as Hirra the One-eyed, a marked hawk ever after, shunned and persecuted by all her kind.

3

As the weeks went by Klee grew in feather and spirit. He was still barely more than half the size of Hirra, but far more alert and active. She, blighted beauty, was growing sleek and lazy, a full-breasted female bigger now than her mother. Perhaps her plumpness, added to her disability, held her back: whatever the reason, it was Klee's turn now to be the forward one. Every morning there was no holding him to the interior of the nest,—in any case by this time it was too trampled, too littered with musty refuse to be sweet or serviceable: he would take great jumps, flapping his wings with exaggerated effort and alighting clumsily on some neighbouring bough, there to chitter loud and long for his mother to come. When she did she would scold him for a great booby, shout a harsh note at him and be off again. Or she would fly in with his prey, perhaps after two hours or more, and stand facing him with it dangling in her bill, challenging him to come and take it. When he tried, she slipped from her perch and glided slowly in front of him, one eye looking behind to see what he would do next. It was a good game, his first full taste of excitement, better by far than having to stay wing-tied in the nest, unable to do more than bob up and down (too nervous to plunge yet yearning to throw himself into a glorious freedom): it was pure play and he took to it easily. At first rewards came quickly, but later on his mother grew capricious, distant, refused to let him catch her up first, second or even the third time: off she would dart like the flies of his fledgling days. Sometimes he grew quite irritable at such treatment. Nor did she now show him any affection. When he *did* manage to alight beside her, her eyes were hard like agate, stone-staring and sparked with white fire, and when he attempted to take the food which she had dropped between her talons she would snatch it up roughly and be off again in a flash. It made him mad. In a fury he urged himself after her, but she twisted beneath him, went curving away between the boles of neighbouring trees, there to titter at him mockingly.

Exhausted by his efforts, Klee perched panting. The speed made his back ache. He was frantic with hunger, baffled with his own helpless spleen : yet there was no resting until he had caught her. In sheer distress he stretched his throat and gave out a shrill rippling whistle, diffident and pleading. It was his first grown utterance, quite distinct from the meaningless sibilances which had punctuated his feeding times in the eyrie days.

From the nest tree he heard his mother's more full-throated answer, an echo almost of his own weak cry, mimicking, mocking, non-committal. A rustle, and there she was, crowning the dead topmost bough like a rusty weathercock, still toying with the remains of some unlucky wrenlet, cocking her head to eye Klee questioningly.

Finding him thus completely balked she next spun round about the tree in which he sat, circled it flauntingly to tempt him ; and then with a strange, harsh cry, flung herself up above him fountain-like, dropped the dead bird almost into his eager gape, then plunged and caught it with a shriek. With an exasperated scream she brushed his face, shot up, up, up beyond his tardy reach. This was too much : in that instant Klee was transformed into a jet of lightning anger. No half-hearted, timorous pursuit now ; he flung himself after her so passionately that every straining feather whirred like wire. Before he knew what was happening he was almost under her tail, could see the red ribbon of flesh dangling there in her tight feet.

Only now his mood had changed. He forgot his furious

hunger, his helpless nervousness. As he rose he felt the strength of the upper air sustaining him, bearing him easily so that he rode upon it comfortably, felt even more at ease than he did when secure on swaying branch. In every quill he felt new confidence, and alternately spreading and closing the firm tips of his wings he gloried in this new delightful ease. He was no longer an amateur: for the first time in his life he revelled in the awareness of his own surprising mastery.

Keee . . . she called wistfully, spiralling softly above him.

Keeeee . . . he answered, gladly following her motions.

For an hour the two sky-skated, drifting in sightless circles, mazy evolutions, wind-silent parabolas which mesmerized Klee's mind with lazy joy. Once she disappeared for a moment into a trailing scarf of cloud, but before its wet chill could touch him it had surged clear and there they were again, two floating alone in an earthless world of light. Circle and wider counter-circle, then circle again, ever higher and higher, thistledown drifting: and all there was to do was to hold wings to the air's strength, relaxed and floating.

This was Klee's first soaring. Clod-bound, earthlings can know nothing of the mysteries of such sky-communion, or the wind-purity of their linked and mystic motions—alone together in a universe of light. Leave them there then together: let air's meaning seep into their feathers, drench them through with limitless freedom. . . .

How long it lasted Klee never knew. For his own part, he might willingly have surrendered himself for ever to the moving cloudland where dream-shapes drifted in gleams and everything, everything was care-free and idle. Losing the earth, he had found himself. Or rather he had lost all feeling, left behind him all sense of fidgeting urgency.

This was pure being. So perfect he could have soared for ever.

His mother, indeed, was the first to tire—or rather to be satisfied. Without warning her wings took on fresh resolution, and letting go the crushed bird from her foot she followed it down.

Surprised, Klee watched her dropping, diminishing to thrush-size, mouse-size, no bigger than a beetle, a bead. He saw her rolling and swaying slightly as the curve of her dive steepened: another moment and she would be gone through the fleecy cloud-floor, lost to his vision. But as he watched, wondering at her deserting him like this, she accelerated headlong, somersaulted and caught the tiny corpse with one upstretching claw as she rolled. And in the same uninterrupted arc flowed up and round on the windy tide.

Hik! she called imperiously. And again, Hik!

Banking, side-slipping, Klee closed his wings reluctantly and followed her down into the darkening fog, through it, out, piercing its greyness till the green chequer-board earth came tilting up to greet him again. For a time he was lost, could not see his mother against the new confusing landscape, until he heard her cry, and there she was, taking her ease again a hundred feet below him. So impetuous was his downrush that he would have struck her, but she avoided him with the slightest twist of her shoulders, then flew alongside. She was still trailing the meat for him to see, but it was not that which riveted his attention now so much as the strangeness in her eye: as though she were perturbed by some trouble indefinable. Once, twice she chattered . . . half angry, half nervous.

Then she dropped it and slid sideways, upwards, out of his vision. As he planed he watched the morsel drop; his eyes fastened on it greedily, saw it more clearly the smaller it grew until they marked where it pitched at last into a tussock of rushes, rolled, lay still: and a wild exhilaration possessed him. He knew what was expected of him. He knew now how to do it. Without trace of hesitancy he clapped both wings tight to his back and stooped cleanly earthwards. His first dive, yet his was the ready-made perfection of an expert: his aim was unwavering, as unerring as a pearl dropping down the taut incline of a string. Never before had he enjoyed such a sensation of ease and power. The field, the stream with its bushes the rushes, all swelled up to meet him. Then as he sensed the warmer grossness of the meadowsweet fragrance streaming thicker in his nostrils, he spread his tail and fetched up abruptly, immediately above the quarry. A bare moment he hung there, poised, then shot out both feet and landed lightly.

Before bending to tear the pulped nape of the dead bird Klee did what he had always done before feeding,—look up and about him. No personal mannerism that. Like all hawks he was gifted with a wild, unsleeping caution. The sky was quite clear, however,—only a few cumbersome rooks straggling homewards. Of his mother there was no sign. No speck in the cloud firmament.

He never saw her again.

4

For a day or two he felt rather lost, left all to himself; but there was always something to occupy his time. Preening, for instance. Eight weeks in the eyrie with nothing much better to do than pluck his itching quills and comb his powdery feathers while he waited to be fed,—this long confinement had seen the formation of a habit which he was never to forget. Morning, after his first meal; afternoon, when he had had his bath and spent an hour sitting in the quiet sun; and evening, just before he curled up to roost,—these were his regular times. With him, preening amounted almost to a religious rite. It took time. First his streaked breast; then twisting his neck in its socket to nibble the barred brown of his mantle; then separating his tail feathers one by one, smoothing the frayed edges: after which he always stretched his wings in luxurious ease, one after the other. How he enjoyed the feel of his splayed pinions, the stiff tips resilient as blades of finest steel! When he was nearly done he half-clenched his foot and scratched his nape vigorously, scrabbled his poll and his face with steel hooks to rid himself of the mites which infested his tight skin. Then he stood up, shook himself vigorously, ruffled all his feathers loose till he looked twice his normal size, then as he let them subside looked about him sharply, in readiness for the next move. Once he had made himself comfortable it was not long before he set off on his questings again.

From now on he played a lone hand. During that first week he was hard put to find a living of any sort. For hours he did nothing but mope, half-expecting his mother's return, but then hunger would not let him doze in inanition:

it made him resolute. Usually something caught his eye as he sat, sometimes on a gate-post by the willow stream: twitching grasshopper or cockroach creeping. Down he dropped and swallowed it. Though meals of this kind were scarcely satisfying they were easily come by, a sure source of supply,—so for a time he became a post-squatter, always peering and prying at the grass beneath him. At the first rustle or grass blade hinting at stirring he grew rigid, crouched; the feathers on his head and back lay back smoothly, his whole posture expressive of anticipation. Then he pounced.

Klee soon grew tired of trifles like these, however. He craved some more full-blooded satisfaction. For a time he tried a loftier look-out, the top of a telegraph pole in the river meadows. Its height enabled him to cover a much greater area of ground, but it had the disadvantage of being conspicuous: he was forever being disturbed by the dangerous passage of men on the road nearby and the harsh yelping of sheep-dogs startled his placid concentration, made him look up in nervous distraction. Often he had to flee hurriedly. Once or twice he saw movements on the mole-hills there, a bank vole washing its sleek face by the stream or shrew scurrying in the rushes, but he had no luck: excitement made him blunder. He would launch out and poise above them, his wings whirring in a flurry of eagerness, but always they were gone without trace. Each time he had to return to his perch without dropping, resume his disconsolate watch for small fry. After a time even this variation palled and he was driven to look for more profitable hunting grounds. It was beginning to dawn on him that a field with a path in it was no place at all,—an odd mole or straying mouse, perhaps,—but for the most part barren ground, better shunned.

Then one day he discovered the oak spinney. It was hidden in a green fold of the cliffs, a deep combe winding inland from the sea, not far from the eyrie where he had been born. Hitherto an unnamed fear had prevented his visiting it. During their first days on the wing together his mother and Hirra had always given it a wide berth, for some reason never made clear,—but that morning Klee had dined well (a windfall of purple beetles), and the attraction of the quiet trees was more than he could resist. Down there it was sheltered from the wind. Ideal for a doze. An open drive threaded the otherwise impenetrable thickness of foliage, through which a hidden trickle of water gurgled mysteriously. The air was thick with the lazy hum of insects about the leaves, and round the wood edge monstrous dragon-flies darted horizontally, emerald, crimson and gold,—spangles of solid fire that stuck an instant in front of his eye, flashed and then shot away.

But it was not dragon-flies which interested Klee. He knew better than to take up their staring challenge; besides, he was feeling lazy this afternoon. Down there on the open floor of the spinney there were movements which he could not quite make out, little cries, too: they made him restive, in spite of his drowsiness. Presently from the lush grass there emerged a small figure, brown, furry, bright-eyed. For a moment it stopped, looked up and squeaked, then darted back into cover.

Klee flattened. His head thrust out, eyes blazing. With his tail shut like a knife he gripped the branch and made ready for it to reappear. Sure enough it did,—and another,—and still another, all squeaking and chirping.

No hesitation now. Gliding out into the sunglare Klee covered the spot on flickering wings, his body tense but all his flight feathers a shimmer, as invisible almost as the electric wings of the dragon-flies. With eyes downthrust he searched for the hidden prey. Either they had heard the swish of his body or seen his black shadow sweeping behind them, for not a chick was now visible. He dropped ten feet and pulled himself up suddenly almost above their hiding-place: then he saw one crouching under a marigold leaf. Loosing his dangling feet Klee flopped all-aheap on the ground and drove his eight talons clean through the soft flesh, shrouding his victim with his dropped wings and bending his head almost to the ground to watch it struggling between his legs and to make quite certain that it did not dodge out in front. The chick squawked for a moment, then lay still. At the first agonized cheep all the others started into sudden life, scattering in all directions through the grass, some running, some half fluttering in their panic retreat. One even fumbled from beneath Klee's wing: for a moment he thought it was his original victim and was so surprised that he could only make a last-minute, ineffectual jab at it as it bolted into the darkness of intertwining roots.

What happened next Klee never knew. In any case words are too slow to describe it. His eye might have caught something of the jolting speed of lightning or held in its retina all the arrowy flight of a kingfisher, but it gave no warning whatever of that sickening blackening blow. A great hen pheasant, a dynamo of fury, had hit him like a rocket. The impact smashed his consciousness in pieces: for a time it was all spinning, a cyclonic flicker of dizzy lights. He was lost, lost in the blackness and there was nothing to catch at, not even himself. . . .

Klee's ancestry stood him in good stead, however. Not for nothing was he falcon-bred with the proud blood of sky-cleavers hot in his body. Even though he had been knocked out by the blind onslaught of the pheasant's ferocity he still had sufficient mechanic sense to roll over on his back and strike up with tearing piston-quick claws and bare his barked mouth in a hiss. When at last he realized what was happening he found himself giving jab for jab, feathers spouting on both sides. He struck at her throat and would have seized it, but her very impetuosity was too much for him: it tore loose as she darted at him, one, two, three, with the stinging point of her beak. He had to press his head right back and thrust upwards with his loose shanks to keep her off, or she would have gouged one of his eyes. Her mood was murderous. Rage at her loss had made her desperate. She drummed him with her bony wings, such a buffeting that even now it blinded him, a whirl of rattling blows until he ached. She tried to trample him with her clumsy great feet, but he held her off with his menacing claws, though once or twice she stamped on his breast and kicked. Her attack was staccato succession of blows from wings, feet and bill: every limb stuttered violence.

Quite suddenly she stopped. She turned, ran a few steps and looked back at him still lying there convulsed and glaring on his back; then, as though struck by something which she had forgotten, she crowed aloud (—and at that sound Klee was more daunted than by all her previous fury), then she went rocketing up between the trees. Unstirring, Klee watched her long tail quivering with the intensity of her effort, watched it trail behind her as she ricocheted into the verdant darkness.

He stood up, fluffed out his loose feathers and, as they settled, relaxed. On his nape and crown each tiny sensitive quill loosened again. He shook himself. Sore, shaken as he was, with blood reddening his pale legs, he had already forgotten the pheasant. Not, of course, that he would not recognize her again,—he was not the one to be caught unprepared a second time, either: but the fight was over. All his excitement was gone.

Klee shook himself again. In the scuffle the dead chick had somehow remained where he left it. He picked it up in his mouth, gave a quick glance round and flew painfully back to his perch. There he stretched the baggy little corpse on the rough lichen, studied it a moment, then steadied it with his claws while with hunched shoulders he stooped down to wrench off the head. He did this with a single powerful twist and tossed it aside. Without pausing he tore open its stringy gizzard and plunged into the warm entrails, pulling them forth, tugging, trying to rive their leathery length into manageable portions. The flesh was watery, no strength in its flavour, but he bolted it eagerly. At least it was more satisfying than insects' blood. This he liked best of all, to stand on his victim, to hold it firmly down while he banqueted in triumph.

Once he looked up, but only to wipe the wet meat from his beak. He was always a clean eater, fastidious almost. He stroked his bill sideways, vigorously, on the roughness of the bark, then scratched his face. The stray morsels he picked up carefully, even the wisps of down. Not a shred was wasted. Then he returned to the carcase, took it firmly in his gape, gulped, gulped again and swallowed it whole. He felt better then.

Round him the gnats spun dreamily, dragon-flies still shimmered and darted. Leaves hung unstirred, glossy with heat, and the hidden runnel below trickled through the summer silence as though nothing could ever disturb it. The whole incident, indeed, had been no more than a flustering moment—a matter of seconds.

Calm on his shaded perch, Klee sat in the dappling screen of the leaves, feeling the satisfying lump of the chick settling inside his choked crop. At times there was a delicate rippling movement in his throat, stirring his feathers, and once he brought up a black mass of beetle shards. For a time they hung from his mouth in a sticky pellet, and he was too lazy to eject them properly; then he waggled his head and let it drop.

For the first time in his life he felt satisfied. There was nothing now to nag him to action or vague discontent: he could just sit and look about him, enjoying the quietness of the noon woodland. A sudden exultation filled him : he raised his throat and gave forth a flute-like rippling whistle. It was the only means he had of expressing his happiness, voicing his wild freedom.

At last, his first real kill!

5

KRARK the old crow yawned. Aged, verminous Krark, good-for-nothing of the cliffs, too far gone even to earn an honest living. For thirty years he had trailed that crumpled claw and cocked his wicked black bead of an eye at all that went on in the neighbourhood, tilting up his raggy tail to caw disapproval. Morose and solitary, he was nobody's friend. Certainly not at the moment.

Kaa! he scraped, and rubbed his thin pate with the stump of his foot.

Kaa! ka!

Flea-midgets crawled unmolested round the dry rims of his tired eyes,—he was too lazy even to scratch. These days even the rankest carrion had lost its interest. His private alcove among the rocks stank of putrid bits that he had stowed away in crannies and then forgotten,—bones of trapped rabbits, dung, an old candle filched from the tide-line, the dried placenta of a dead ewe . . .

His only solace now was in mischief. He resented anything in the nature of intrusion in what he had come to consider his own private domain. After all, his thirty years' residence had bred in him a certain feeling of ownership; and this newcomer to the cliff, this swaggering youngster of a hawk, had to be taught a lesson.

Krark yawned again, clicked his bill and considered. In cunning ways and trouble-making tricks he had no equal. Not even that still more ancient seer, Ronka the Raven, could contrive more tortuous plans,—but then Ronka was venerable and well-preserved, not a cross-grained tattered cripple like Krark.

Looking down, he could see the young hawk sunning

itself on the topmost spray of a rowan tree which sprouted out from a cleft half-way down the crag. Further down still, where the surf spouted green and white, a group of statuesque shags were holding conclave, writhing their satin, meagre necks and ceremoniously conversing,—but that was nobody's business. All the sea-birds lived a life apart, unaccountable; a queer lot altogether. A hawk was another matter; an unwanted newcomer, a nuisance,—possibly even a menace. Anyway, he had to be got rid of somehow; to every crow it was an understood thing that all hawks should be harried at all times,—at least the small and inoffensive ones. This stripling would be easy game.

But how?

Krark was too stiff and slow a-wing to tackle him unaided. At the best of times the old crow creaked as he laboured overland, and in such a sea-breeze as this he knew the kestrel would easily outride him, make his slow awkward pursuit look foolish in a moment. He knew better than attempt it. In any case he was far, far too tired for anything so strenuous.

There were other ways, however. Cocking up his tail he bowed deeply forward and barked again, more angrily this time:

Krakra! krakra!

Then he walked gravely forward, rolling slightly from side to side, and perching on pinnacle awaited the approach of reinforcements. He had not long to wait. Presently his dim, sidelong vision marked the approach of three more crows. Attracted by his voice they came flapping round the headland, playing the fool with each other and ready for any diversion. Just what he had expected. Three young fools straight out of the nest,—what could be better? They were no friends of Krark—indeed, their father and he had been sworn enemies in many a long springtime,—but where a hawk is concerned all crows make common cause.

As the three drew nearer Krark launched himself out above the water and struggled through the first boisterousness of the conflicting wind. In his one foot he clasped a white pebble, an old and favourite plaything of his, rescued time and again to be stored among his other treasures in the alcove. He made over to where Klee sat, calling hoarsely again and again, then when almost directly overhead he dropped the stone, tumbled over in mid-air, caught it again and repeated the manœuvre. It was an old trick, the only one he knew in fact, but it served.

To say that Klee was not thinking of anything would be meaningless (—he never did),—and to say that he was taken by surprise would be inaccurate (—he never was); but just at that moment his mood was relaxed. He was not dozing, not drowsy even, though he had only now come from the spinney with two more pheasant chicks inside him: he was just taking things easy, waiting for them to settle more comfortably. The rowan-tree was a new idea of his. It was a safe place at all times of the day, provided good look-out, and the curving headland sheltered it from the blast of the open sea. Recently he had taken to roosting in a cranny in the cliff above it.

His breast feathers were fluffed out now in a broad and comfortable waistcoat, and with one foot drawn up into the warmth he balanced firmly on the other, taking his ease. His head rested slightly to one side, the downward eye slowly blinking. With the other, almost as aimless, he noted the whole white space of the sky controlled for the time by a single dark shape,—Peea the huge buzzard, drifting like a kite. An old boor, Peea, and a great coward, despite those enormous vans.

Klee's throat contracted. For a moment it swelled,—he looked as though the paroxysm would choke him,—then his mouth gaped, wide as a frog's, and he brought up a long pellet, a sticky mass compact of bones, down and beetle-backs. Or rather he brought up half. With that great mouthful protruding, the remainder stuck in his throat, he felt rather helpless; still he made no effort to rid himself of the indigestible lump. He let it dangle. No hurry.

Presently Peea folded back her ample wingspan and glided down into the shadow of the cliff, mewing anxiously as she came, and Klee saw why. Far up, higher even than the moving intervening clouds, a pair of silver crosses were sailing in the blue. The sunlight gilded their pallid under-wings: their breasts glinted like brooches. It was Hek and his mate Hikka, the princely peregrines. But they were only playing,—Peea was always a fretful, timorous old thing. Still, every flying thing did well to pay them deference, for when falcons were abroad you could never tell what might happen: they claimed the sky as their monopoly. They were touchy, too, their moods unaccountable; and when their sudden anger blazed it might vent itself on anything, a buzzard even. Nor was there any escaping such lightning execution.

Krrrog! barked the raven, ominous in his cave.

No, perhaps after all, Peea was wise. Far better to hug the earth.

It was at this moment that Klee was aware of the crow tumbling above him. He had already marked his approach with an indifferent eye, had taken no notice of his first crazy gestures above the rowan. Mangy Krark,—only a filthy old crow. Best ignore him.

But Krark did not intend to be ignored. Descending, he began dropping and catching the stone more quickly than ever, almost in the hawk's face. Ka! ka! ka! ka! he shrieked in mock alarm, voicing his execration with exaggerated care. He knew how to be importunate, how to attract a crowd of persecutors, and start a hawk-hunt. Trust Krark!

Klee sat tight. He was more puzzled than irritated by

this unprovoked interference with his leisure. Why couldn't Krark leave him alone? To have such a decrepit rascal mock him like this, taunt him to his face! He ejected the rest of the pellet and shifted on to both feet uneasily, ruffling himself. From time to time he flinched. The stone kept dropping nearer and nearer: once the crow's worn wing almost struck him on the cheek, causing him to snap at it viciously. Krark shrieked again, a squawk of real alarm this time.

It was enough. Attracted by the commotion the three young crows, which had so far been hanging around wondering what it was all about, now came hurrying, eager to join in the fray. Without hesitation they began swooping and diving on the crouching hawk, trying to drive him from his position of security. There was little skill or method in their attack, but it was bewildering in its violence. They kept driving at him from behind, making him twist and turn his head in every direction to protect himself from their horny bills. To make matters worse a troop of daring missel-thrushes had settled in the branches, churring at him angrily, doing their best to chivvy him. For a trice his attention was divided,—and in that confused instant one of the crows fetched him a clout on the head,—only a half-hearted buffet, but it almost overtoppled him.

Karrr! cried Krark, goading them on to fresh efforts.

The situation was fast becoming unbearable. The more he ducked and twisted, the more persistent grew their harryings; and the noise was terrific. Loth as he was to leave his point of vantage, he had to escape their attentions somehow. Clearly they would not leave off pestering him so long as he stayed. What had begun as mere baiting, a game, had now become serious. There was deadly anger in their thrusts.

With sudden cleaving Klee sped up into the air, leaving behind the clamorous thrushes and slow Krark in a gush of wind. He climbed swiftly, breasting the land breeze and allowing it to carry him over towards the hills: but one of the crows was already above him. He had the advantage from the start and meant to maintain it, calling on his fellows to assist him. Already Klee had outdistanced them, but this fellow was not so easily shaken off. Each time he came blundering at him Klee merely tilted a wing and avoided him easily, not even troubling to drop his talons in self-defence: the crow would be the first to tire, he knew. After each attack he spread his wings and glided in a serene arc, even beginning to note the details of the earth beneath with an eye to an alternative resting-place when this fray was all over; but then his assailant redoubled his efforts, came pelting down upon him with renewed fury. Caught in the middle of his idle planing Klee refused to be too much upset, prepared only a languid sideslip; but he had taken too much for granted. The crow jerked aside, too, and grappled him in mid-air, forcing him over on his back so that the two of them fell interlocked. Over and over they tumbled, Klee trying furiously to free himself, trying to get his claws into those hateful black legs. Madly he tore at the crow's bony chest. It muttered hoarsely and let go—and in a flash Klee was streaming headlong earthwards, in terror, for his eye had seen something of which the baffled crow was still unaware. Even through the thick of the fight Klee had heard the exultant yelp of the tiercel,—it had added to his desperation,—and as he plummeted down he could see the winged thunderbolt screaming after him,—overtaking . . .

It was Hikka, mad for a kill. Her powerful body, a wedge of steel, was aimed after him like a bullet: she did not just dive, but propelled herself earthwards with fanatical wing-slashes, swaying slightly, rhythmically as she shot at her objective. Down, down, down, down, with the abandoned recklessness of shooting star, she whistled across the sky, bigger, bigger, bigger . . . He could hear the air streaming through her tense feathers.

Terrified, he urged what little speed he could still muster. But at the last moment Hikka levelled, swerved in her purpose without losing a fraction of her wild momentum. Klee heard the last-minute cry of the flopping crow, the dead thud of impact, the choked squawk of agony. . . . She had felled him with one sledge-hammer stroke, tearing his back open; and in the same movement was winging back to her approving mate. A hundred feathers hung suspended in the upper air, scattering and slowly falling—like charred bits of burnt paper.

Klee hurtled into the darkness of a holly bush, burst right inside. His eyes were wider than usual. His wings twitched fitfully. Through the sheltering leaves he saw the limp body of the crow falling brokenly, still a long way up, a lax bundle. Next minute it crashed through the branches of a tree nearby, hung for a moment caught, then dropped into the long grass by the rivulet's edge, where it lay in a spatter of blood.

Later Krark found it there and picked out both the eyes.

6

After that Klee abandoned his cliff roost. The rowan-tree knew him no more. He had had enough of crows for the time being and made his night quarters now in the spinney,—one place in which, for some reason, no crow ever ventured. Every evening he returned thither, soaring over the wood at a great height first to be sure that all was well, then dropping down into its dark shelter. There was an old magpie's nest in the top of one of the oaks; a rickety structure with most of its domed roof long since fallen in, the twig-lining soft with mildew, but on most nights tolerably snug. Most important of all, he had so far not been disturbed there.

Before retiring he went through his usual ablutions. Feather by feather he made himself neat and comfortable, ruffled himself and stood for a time on one leg. Gradually he subsided into a sitting posture, turning himself to suit the filtering wind. Next he screwed his head round towards his tail and buried it between the warmth of his shoulders, shifting it twice or thrice and looking up again before finally settling. When this was done all his quills would arch up until he looked as round as a ball, a mound of luxurious feathers with only the tail protruding. Then he knew no more.

Once in the darkness he wakened to find himself confronted by a glaring shape,—an owl with face afire was standing erect above him. Before he had time to stir, it uttered a strange wavering cry which broke off in a dry ruttle of surprise as it saw him. As he withdrew his head the cold gleam of those twin circles changed from gold to satanic green, but he need not have troubled; the creature disappeared as softly as it had come. At times the wood was full of weird owl-music, sad quavering flute-notes answering one another. Harmless creatures.

Klee was not the earliest of risers.

In the early mornings he was often roused by scampering squirrels. They had a nest somewhere at hand and were for ever skiftering about in the branches, leaping and running and chattering nonsense to each other. Some of the young ones had not yet accustomed themselves to his new tenancy and more than once ran full tilt into him, fetching up with a terrified squeak when they realized their error. When that happened the whole family would assemble just out of reach and shout abuse at him from a safe branch, not that he felt inclined to stay there, once awakened. He shook himself, arched both wings to their utmost overhead and set off on the long day's quest.

He had long since given up taking pheasant chicks. For one thing they had by this time grown too big for him and for another he was by nature not enamoured of bird-flesh,—tame, soft stuff: the feathers caught in his bristles, stuck in his mouth annoyingly. Give him something solid and satisfying, something with fur to thicken it! Besides, he had no need of thieving ways. He was not a treacherous sneak like those wood cousins of his, the sparrow-hawks,—always on the watch, ready to dash out of covert or corner to pounce on unsuspecting linnets. Klee's place was the sky. Above all else he loved its wide freedom;—hunting or playing, his pleasance was there alone. And by this time he had learned the hunter's trade. Already there was not a trick of it he did not know.

There was method in Klee's hunting. Each morning he rose, testing the feel of the wind, learning first what the day's prospects were to be. For an hour or so he reconnoitred, surveying the stretch of land which he was slowly coming to call his own. There was none to challenge him hereabouts, it seemed: not since he left the eyrie had he seen any sign of his parents or of Hirra—or, for that matter, of any other kestrel. So much the better.

It was good hunting ground too, well stocked, far better than the flat riverside and village fields which he had tried in the early days. To begin with there was, inland, beyond the spinney, a mile or more of rising waste,—a wide common facing across to the far sea-horizon. Large areas of it were impassable tangles of thorn and gorse scrub, but there were free spaces of lawn close-cropped by wandering sheep. The bushes provided just the necessary screen,—it was easy to drop *behind* the unsuspecting victim, his tell-tale shadow hidden in the morning shadows of the branches, the swish of his descent mingling with the stirring leaves,—and then dash upon it diagonally before it had time to run. Not his approved style of making a kill, but he had had one or two shrews and many a basking lizard that way. The common was his first beat every morning.

This waste land rose gradually to a fir-crowned hillock (ideal watch-tower at noon), then fell away behind into a broad valley of fields and marsh. There was a hazel lane meandering from the beach and one or two houses; but though there was usually no one about, he avoided these, despite the temptation of the telegraph poles. He might cast an envious eye at the swarm of yellow chicks crowding the field at the back of the farmhouse, but he left them severely alone as he swung high over to the marsh. Anything connected with human affairs was suspect,—he never gave it a single thought,—he led his own life. Sometimes as he passed that way he saw a woman waving her apron, scattering corn to the nodding hens: or there was washing on the line, strange shapes leaping and flapping dangerously. The whole place filled him with disquiet and foreboding. Klee hated anything white.

The marsh, on the contrary, was pure delight. Not that

it was easy to work. Most of it was overgrown with thick rush-spikes which grew as tall as shrubs, providing impenetrable cover, but there were boggy patches where the naked peat bared its black flesh to view. In the centre the ground was wet and spongy, a black pool framed with flowers. Lemon-petalled flags stood stiffly up, bullrush pokers and reed-spears,—the edges a riot of loose-strife and pink ragged-robin. What attracted Klee, however, was an upright post driven into the bare mud, the only convenient resting-place in the whole expanse of that wilderness.

And a resting-place was needed. Some days he would fly up and down a dozen times, quarter every corner of the marsh without his survey yielding as much as a morsel. If it rained, or if the wind were wrong, perhaps not a creature stirred from its hole and the hawk had to give up in the end. In the end . . . for Klee was nothing if not painstaking. He went about his work with a massive patience. An unfailing, uncomplaining thoroughness sustained his long search,—he was never entirely without hope,—but even a falcon's wings grow weary. At such times the pool post was his armchair: he used to sit there and wait for frogs or try picking tadpoles from the wriggling shallows. A messy business, but it kept him going.

The great thing about the marsh was that when something did turn up,—and not every day was unlucky,—it was more than worth while. The tall rushes were peopled by a colony of dark-skinned voles, a type Klee had not seen elsewhere, smooth, round-bodied, and most tasty. Some of the older ones were big, too, almost the size of rats, only much easier to kill. So far he had not caught more than one or two of these,—the others had all been incautious youngsters,—but a meal of one was enough to satisfy him for a day. He ate them on the spot, for there was never anything to disturb him there. Though he liked to take his time, picking out first the back of the neck as a sample, then tearing the head off, the guts out, swallowing the fur tatters, he preferred best of all a solid cropful at the end before the corpse-blood had quite cooled. If the last bones were quite unmanageable,—often they jammed in his throat for all his straining,—he might leave them, but usually he carried off the remains to his post, there to pick them clean at greater leisure.

Starved or replete, the pool was his regular haunt at midday. The shy sedge warblers might emerge to chide him, straddling the reed stems and opening their little red mouths in anger at his presence, or the furtive moorhens croak anxiously, shepherding their woolly chicks, but he scarcely heard them. It was a place of peace.

Still, he could not sit snoozing there all day, however comfortable he might be feeling. There was always the sky's attraction pulling him like a magnet, the upward impulse urging him to resume his wanderings. His whole existence was a prolonged restlessness. While he was crop-crammed his hankerings might for a time be stilled, but that never lasted long: his digestion was so swift that even the top-heaviest vole melted away inside him in an afternoon.

The common and the marsh provided his regular grounds, but there was, further afield, an indeterminate hinterland to which he now came with gathering frequency,—the moor. He had not yet explored it thoroughly, and he had quite enough to do beating and rebeating the bounds of his own peculiar domain; nevertheless its vastness intrigued him. If he struck lucky early in the day he felt free to do a little travelling on his own account,—and the heather had obvious possibilities. There were shrews,—in places the ground was riddled with them,—short-tailed mice and infant rabbits that sat sleeping in the sun, easy game. And though the wind up there was often troublesome there were stone walls rambling up the slopes, deserted sheep-pens on which to sit and preen. Klee still liked an after-lunch dessert of beetles, too, and there were hundreds everywhere,—the heather was alive with them, crawling from stone to stone. Just a matter of sitting and waiting . . . he took his pick as he felt like it.

How far did he travel in the course of his gipsy day? Klee took no account of distance. The moor summit, the limit so far of his explorations, was, raven-wise, four miles from the beach, but he inspected every yard of the countryside intervening, tracing sky-squares and -triangles again and again in his surveys until he knew every hole and hiding-place. By evening his mazy flight might have carried him two hundred miles, maybe three.

It was afternoon, a sunny autumn day. In the morning there had been a cold sea-fret shrouding the cliffs and rolling inland over the grey common. Even a hawk's eye was baffled by its filming whiteness, so for once he flew straight over to the marsh. It was not much better there; he had to drop low, starting up the squeaking larks and meadow pipits as he swept the rush-tippets,—a novel manœuvre which brought an immediate reward, a slow mole poking its wrinkling snout to the raw air, still scrabbling the earth away from its rheumy pin eyes. He slewed round and seized it before it had time to think of withdrawal. The meat was tough and dry, but he finished it, then sat and preened for an hour by the pool. Then he had his bath,—a vigorous dousing and splashing in one of the water-filled hollows of the peat. How he ducked and revelled in it! beat the water with furious wings, opened all his feathers and threw it on to his back, let it stream and trickle down his breast. By the time he was done he had become a bedraggled, skinny-looking creature, a wreck of his former sleek self: but he felt freshened, ready for anything. When he had had enough, of course, he had to return to the post, there to sit and dry himself in the wind, get himself perfectly groomed. After which he felt free to roam.

It was still early in the day. The sun had just broken through, spreading its yellow shield across the lightening green expanse. The last low clouds were departing, sweeping immense shadows of indigo across the level marsh in front of them, trailing, wreathing themselves around the shoulders of the hills and pouring over into the vague distances beyond. It was quite warm now, calm. He set off for the moors.

As he rose he soared. The sea first, with its misted headlands one by one, came up to greet him, then the cloud-shapes of mountains far inland, hanging like himself in mid-air, alluring, violet-pale: but these were not for him, only the circling landscape spread beneath. Every detail was clear. As he approached the higher ground he felt the benefit of the freshening air currents and, in an idle mood, allowed himself to be borne by them. Drifting, he all but dozed, careening lazily or shifting one wing to change his direction, more for amusement than for any better purpose. That afternoon he might have lost himself entirely in that bright sky, had not his attentions been attracted by the presence of others in it. Far below he saw Peea and her two umber-backed sons disporting: like Klee, they too had fed well, evidently, and were taking gentle exercise. Half nervously, half curiously he planed over towards them. The old buzzard held a spray of dried seaweed in her feet; she kept dropping it and catching it again with legs outstretched,—rather like Krark's trick,—while the two youngsters, huge creatures, flew round her whining and squawling. Their wings were far too big for them. What maladroit louts they were! Such an ample span of pinions was all very well for soaring, but at close quarters or in an emergency it left them floundering. Klee could see that by the way they tumbled on their backs, toppled sideways ludicrously, their scraggy legs clawing frantically as they tried to take that plaything,—and he despised them.

Choosing his moment carefully he went boring in amongst them,—no falcon's stoop, but with a show of determination that took them off their guard. They had not seen him coming. He made straight at the nearer of the young buzzards, causing it to throw back in alarm, almost twisting its quills out in the effort to avoid Klee's onset.

Geeeahyak! squealed Peea as the slight hawk came shooting up beneath her tail. Then as he swerved,—for her dangerous feet were ready for him,—she somersaulted, but he was past her, looping at the third buzzard. In a moment he had thrown them all into utter confusion, for he was in and out again before they could turn, like an eel among whales. Not that he meant any mischief: but his athletic sport was too much for them,—the young birds broke and scattered, ploughing off seawards and crying piteously as they fled. For a time he followed Peea, teasing her to drop the seaweed, but she, crotchety thing, avoided him and kept tight hold. Once when he all but grazed her broad back she struck at him viciously. He left her to follow her offspring back to the cliffs. Then he resumed his minute inspection of the moor.

He pulled up, winnowing rapidly. A movement. Something strange stirring. He watched it, hanging motionless as if suspended from an invisible thread, balancing so still that he scarcely breathed. Then he winnowed again, wings awhirr. This was exciting! Again he hung, steadying himself to make certain of the queer creature which had ventured forth. Then he closed his wings and plunged vertically, twenty, thirty feet, then braked suddenly with fanned tail, hovering again. His chest-bone leaned on the wind, breasting it as smoothly as the finest keel in water. This needed careful handling, for the late sun cast his flickering shadow in front. A false move and the quarry would be gone in a flash. He swayed sideways slightly, pendulous, took the breeze more abeam, and dropped again.

He was almost in striking distance. And what a strange, evil thing this was! But it was too late now to cry off. Still, there was something sinister in its sloth. Its stony head was raised menacingly, its lipless mouth twitching at him, but it made no effort to escape. Klee poised, hesitated, then flung himself on the snake.

For the first time since his encounter with the hen pheasant he got a shock. At the first pinch of his claws the adder became electric. Its tail lashed round his body, pulled him down: its head twisted and darted in his face and it hissed abominably. But he held it firmly, seized it by the neck and squeezed for dear life. Still it squirmed. He had not previously known anything like this. Usually they squeaked a little and then lay still, but not this one. The tighter he held it the more violent its efforts became; it whipped him savagely, swelled under him like elastic, forcing him over on his side. His one free wing flayed the air frantically as it pinned him, then in desperation he wrenched free the other and struggled into the air still clutching his enemy. No letting go now. . . . The heaving weight of it was almost too much for him, but he limped along, getting higher as the slope fell away, bending almost double to slash its head to ribbons. Still it writhed. But the further he flew its struggles grew weaker and more intermittent until at last only the tail quivered convulsively: then even that hung limply. . . .

As he crossed the farm fields homeward bound he was set upon by a bevy of clamorous rooks, themselves on a similar errand. To avoid them he jettisoned the dead snake and swung wearily aside. He watched their clumsy efforts to intercept the strange object, loosely twirling, coiling as it fell,—but they were far too slow and lost interest before it even reached the ground. It fell at the back of the house, quite close to a grazing horse, which approached it suspiciously, sniffed, then kicked its hind legs and bolted.

Wearily Klee circled over the sleepy spinney, his wings burnished by the last high shafts of the sunken sun, then he sank through the soft air of the evening, soothed by its moist coolness, glad at the feathery trees uprushing to receive him.

Churruk! said the magpie, cocking its poker tail apprehensively on the fence.

Skrark! screamed the indignant jay, flashing its amethyst-studded wings as it plunged into covert. There were no rabbits.

But Klee was too far gone to take much notice. He made straight for his roost, skimmed the oak tops and turned as usual into the open drive,—almost in the faces of two great men! With a horrified rattle of quills he swerved, but even in that moment of terror he caught the quick glint of deadly steel swivelling at him through the branches and twisted again. A brilliant flash, a roar that blasted the air . . . it flung him among the whistling branches, stung him with fiery points. He would have fallen but he heard their raucous shouts . . . a wild fear exploded all round him but somehow he burst clear. His wing hurt him a great deal, and there was a dull soreness in his side which dragged him down. He could hear them pounding the earth as they ran, the branches crackling, fierce dogs, shouts, another roar of scarlet, the whine of pellets impotently pursuing him.

Terror snatched him like a leaf in the wind.

Somehow he escaped. But his mad retreat had been quite blind. It had carried him down-valley towards the sea. He was too weak to climb and as he fought passionately along, his stricken wing stiffened, grew unmanageable until at last it seized up altogether and he pitched sprawling among the rocks. There he lay spreadeagled, done-for, his chin caught in a cleft and his eyes wide-staring, sightless. Blood stained the stones, grew sticky, matted his feathers, yet still he did not stir. When at last he did he was moved by a burning anger. He had lost all fear. He neither understood nor cared what had happened to him, but these torn holes in his body, this helpless futile wing,—they infuriated him. He pecked at each gunshot wound as savagely as if it were filth that smirched his plumage. It was all wrong, and though the pain was a trifle it would not let him alone. Neither would he cease worrying it.

It was almost dark now. The sea-roar grew louder, the spray crept nearer, white leapings, flashing of water. A gull yelped at him crouching there, then glided ghost-like, faded into the night murk.

Klee slept.

7

FOR three days he could do no more than skulk about the tideline, halt and miserable, nursing his injuries. Fortunately for him the sea cove was all but inaccessible to men, so that he was able to recuperate undisturbed and take things easy.

Not quite undisturbed, however. At high tide the rocks were the immemorial snoozing ground for hundreds of pied oyster-catchers. The first swirl or eddy of the changeful sea was enough to send one or two of them hurrying from their far mudflats to be sure of their place,—for when all were assembled they were packed like limpets on the rocks and late-comers just had to seek elsewhere.

Curious birds, those oyster-catchers, their moods as unaccountable as March winds, yet always vivid and lively. The first day they found him there what a to-do they made! —the whole convocation rippling with nervous excitement, dancing up into the air, settling, then dancing up again as though the dried seaweed were redhot under their toes. It was some time before they accommodated themselves to the idea of his presence there, and even then one or two would come running nervously to watch him, tilting atop a stone at him, pointing their flaming scarlet bills and whistling dubiously. When they saw that he did not so much as move their anxiety changed to curiosity: they ran two or three steps on their long shanks, stopped, blinked a ruby eye at one another and looked puzzled. Often their confused emotions got the better of them,—for want of any better response they began quixotic displays, bending their heads to the sand and trilling softly with suppressed excitement, running after each other tail to tail, all piping in the most foolish manner.

Klee watched them dully. He just sat there, a hunched bundle of dishevelled feathers, and waited. If the tide had been higher the last curling wave would have plucked him from his place without him struggling or caring. His right wing was dead and numb: he had more sense than try to use it. It drooped useless at his side and he made no effort to hitch it into place, only bending his neck occasionally to pick at the raw place under his armpit. He felt weak, without spirit, urgeless. For two days not a morsel had entered his crop. The rock on which he had first alighted was now white with his droppings,—he had not moved from it. It was as much as he could do to balance himself. Often his glazed mind drifted off in a vague stupor, to be abruptly riveted again by some movement close at hand,—a wheatear flicking its white rump as it shot past,—or rock-pipits jerking their way round the margins of salt-pools, looking like mice. Klee was so still,—and they so intent, searching the wet tangles,—that they passed close under him quite oblivious. He did not even turn his head to follow their creeping progress. . . . Statue-still, he maintained his broken posture.

So still he was, indeed, that even Ronka twirling and somersaulting a thousand feet above him was fooled for a moment and came down to prospect. The old raven was quite sure that it was a fresh corpse, ready perhaps for picking, but first he took up a position on the cliff top from which to examine it at a safe distance. First he turned one eye, then the other, meditating: then with a dry comment in his black throat flew slowly down to the beach. No movement. Gravely the dark undertaker waddled nearer; but suddenly he caught the glint of Klee's eye and jumped a foot high in the air, he was so startled.

Kronk! he exclaimed. And without more ado he made off along the cliffs, croaking in disgust.

Perhaps it was this incident which saved Klee's life; but for it he might have sunk beyond recovery. Somehow it called him back to something like alertness. He revived. Somewhere inside him a hidden reserve of energy braced him. He stood up, stretched himself, pecked his wincing wing more tenderly, then started to preen for the first time since his accident.

Not too soon either. Half-way through his toilet he left off, his eye attracted by a restless movement on the sloping cliff above him. An animal about his own size and colour was weaving and darting between the clusters of sea-pinks, now lost from view, now emerging abruptly to snuff the air enquiringly. A hunting stoat. There was something curiously fascinating about its inconsequent motions: it sneaked along belly to the earth like someone lost, wandering in a dream, with the air of a creature searching distractedly for a forgotten hiding-place. There was no taking eyes away from it. Every moment it stopped, doubled back in its tracks, then made off at a tangent, went back again: it made circles, stood up pawing the air with its silky forelegs, showing its shrewd white face, then flattened like a rat and came on again,—and all without a pause, with a supple snaking motion. What was it up to? However intently Klee watched it, there was no reading a meaning in its behaviour, yet there was something about its action which was at once evil and attractive.

Gradually the stoat's meanderings brought it nearer. It was working down towards the beach, still darting from side to side. Presently it made a little run and stopped on the clay slope almost opposite him, its white whiskers twitching, its upturned wet nose wrinkling sensitively: he could not understand why it did not see him. It might easily have leapt across at him. And Klee, from the moment he caught sight of it, had been petrified, not with fear but with a sudden rigidity. His foot was caught in the air, in the very act of scratching his ear: his head was still twisted. . . .

Then he saw why. Prancing in the air above was a crowd of excited rock pipits. The sea-light flickered brassily on their vibrant wings as they hovered, rising and falling geyser-like, a hesitant fountain of birds: and all the while they kept up a continuous, helpless squeaking, opening and shutting their scarlet mouths, clicking their weak bills. They were not mobbing the stoat as they would have done Klee, had they noticed him sitting there alone. Like him, they were puzzled and attracted—and strangely helpless. Lower they came and lower. One, dropping lower than the rest, made a dart at the stoat's humped back, causing it to rear up, its face grimacing, gibbering, fangs bared; but for an instant only. Once again it returned to its crazy wanderings. The squeakings overhead grew more excited than before and still the pipits danced, bounced like puppets jerked on strings.

After a time the hunter came to the level sand. And now its method grew madder even than before. It began running,—gliding, rather, in a mazy, drunken circle: as if trying to catch up with itself. Round, round, round, round, round: then it stopped, faced about and resumed its careerings in the opposite direction. A circle of furry magic. Perching on rocks, the pipits settled all round to watch this weird performance. Wider it wound and wider, while they, answering its lure, came dipping near to watch it. Not once did the stoat stop to look up, while they, suspecting no guile, drew closer: a ring of admirers. Without warning the creature pirouetted, shot sideways and pinned one of the gapers under his flashing paws: there was a scuffle, but in a trice he had it firmly in his jaws. At once the charm was broken. The quiet squeakings changed to piercing shrieks of anger and terror as the pipits scattered and fled. But the show was over,—they did not stay to watch the epilogue to this tragedy.

Left to itself, the stoat dropped the pipit between its paws and licked its bloody chops with silent satisfaction. It had still not noticed the hawk sitting there, five yards away. Now it picked up the dead bird in its mouth and came trotting towards the rock. Its short forelegs moved mincingly, leaving no imprint on the soft sand. Its head was so close to the ground and its eyes so forward-focused that it would certainly have passed beneath without noticing.

But as the creature sidled under, almost brushing him with its tail tippet, Klee's horror and aversion vented itself in a cry.

Kikikikik!

Looking up, the stoat saw him glaring full-face, transfixed with wild aversion. Without stopping to think, it dropped its burden and made off behind the rocks. It reappeared a moment later,—evidently it had thought better of it,—but at the sight of Klee's bared bill and threatening stance it took fright and disappeared for good.

When all was quiet again Klee stooped to examine this lucky windfall. Hopping down, he retrieved it from the pool into which it had fallen, plucked it and ate it with evident relish. Afterwards he washed himself in the brine, —he hated the sticky water, but it was better than no bath at all,—and began to feel something like his old self again. It was still too early for him to attempt anything strenuous with his wing, but he could feel the torn muscles reviving. He even perked up sufficiently to be interested in the leaping sand-hoppers and caught one or two for amusement. They tasted bitter, not sweet like the moor beetles, but he made do with them. He began pursuing them on foot, not a dignified proceeding, but he found that he could scamper quite quickly when he had to,—quite quick enough to seize them before they could spring sideways. The exercise revived him. By the fourth day he had sufficiently recovered to be able to take flying jumps from one rock to another—rather after the style of his first efforts in the eyrie. At times he forgot his injury altogether and in his eagerness aimed himself at the sky: but the wing would not answer,—he found himself grovelling on the sand, wondering what had happened, flapping his free wing in impotent fury.

As it healed, however, he only grew more restless and discontented. True, he was able now to make his way about the lower cliffs almost at will,—and the tide line was not without its interests: one day he found the remains of a dead pigeon there and gorged until he could eat no more, —but the urge to be a-wing again tortured him incessantly. In his blood he could feel the itching change of the season. He could hear its message in the swallows' voices hawking flies along the cliff-tops, in the slow plaintiveness of the redbreast's song,—the robin that came bobbing among the stones looking for sand-fleas like himself. Every night now the darkness was pierced by the cries of migrating birds, night-travellers calling to each other from star to star. Every morning there were newcomers resting for a brief hour or so on the sheltering beach,—dainty wagtails, didapping and trotting from pool to pool, larks, buntings, linnets, sprightly finches of all kinds. They passed on and he remained. Every noontide the bay was traversed by endless streams of white birds, south-bound and idly drifting,—coral-billed terns with pearly pointed wings: they floated like snowflakes. The oyster-catchers were now no longer sole occupiers of the sea-hemmed reef. Lanky godwits mingled in their ranks and burly curlews crowded them out, jostling them. Far out to sea a smoky cloud of waders went undulating over the horizon, now a myriad-shimmer of lights, now a black locust swarm as they turned in their racing flight. Gannet giants, each a dazzle of whiteness, wandered and swung across the bay: and gulls . . .

Gulls of all kinds and colours, of every shape and size,—from the dove-like gentle kittiwakes to the solitary black-backs, great butchers for ever circling overhead, casting long shadows as they prowled, and laughing a gruff sardonic laugh. Klee raised an apprehensive eye at these buccaneers more than once in a day. The smaller black-headed gulls were everywhere, standing in groups in the slack tide or squawling and chasing for scraps, or standing knee-high in pools, their legs marking quick time in the water as they waited for sand-worms to appear: he took no notice of them. Of the blackbacks, however, he was rather afraid—and not for nothing. One morning, maybe a week after his accident, he was sitting in the sun as usual, on the look-out for sand-hoppers, when a pair of them spotted him. He knew by their deep-throated commentary that they were up to something and at once began a nervous nodding of his head, looking from side to side for some bolt-hole. There was none. Their slow cunning made him feel more than helpless.

One of the huge brutes had already alighted and begun walking slowly towards him, in an offhanded, laconic way, which only made its intentions more obvious. The other still planed overhead, grunting from time to time. With one eye Klee marked the insidious approach of the male; the other followed the shadowing flight of the second gull. If they were hoping to catch him off his guard. . . . He could see their brutal beaks yawning hungrily, horn-yellow, spotted with scarlet as if they had been dipped in blood; and he made ready. Not too soon, either, for suddenly there was a rush of air behind him and the female came driving down at him, trying to rush him from his perch, bundle him towards her mate and confederate. All he did was duck, but the very wind of her passing was almost enough to overbalance him. He steadied himself and prepared to meet the second onslaught.

Sure enough, down she came at him, straight out of the sun, but Klee faced her this time and struck out pluckily at her broad white belly as she skimmed him. Disconcerted by this show of spirit, she flew higher, croaking to herself all the time. By this time her mate had edged even nearer and stood ogling impudently at him, not sure whether to fall upon him straight or wait until his mate could contrive an opening, distract his attention for a moment. The hawk was disabled,—they had watched him limping about for days now: and now that he had been meekly sitting there for an hour or more they had expected to put an end to him easily.

Again she swooped, screamed as she passed him, but with no better effect—and again and again. Once, however, he was compelled to scatter: and in that unguarded moment the sly cob took wing and dashed him with an exultant shout. It was the moment for which all three had been waiting . . . and still Klee managed to have the best of it. With an agonized twist of his hurt wing he avoided a collision, managed to flap somehow on to the cliff slope and face them there in something like a position of security.

Finding their chosen victim more nimble than they had expected, the blackguards withdrew, though for some time afterwards they hung about, paraded up and down the cliff-face giving vent to their discontent.

By such a chain of lucky circumstances Klee managed to survive: he lived when others would have been obliterated.

Soon he was taking short flights from rock to rock, arching his wings and gliding delicately, though still afraid to trust himself too far. Then in an afternoon of gale he was caught up willy-nilly and found himself spiralling up with the wind, remembered the green fields again and trees that had changed colour since last he had seen them.

8

OCTOBER filled the lanes with broken sticks. The hedges were choked with the year's debris, and stubble straws flung from fields and haystacks caught and hung in the whistling telegraph wires. A time of tumult and of change.

Klee felt uneasy.

For a month he had led a vagabond career with no proper beat of his own, no regular roost, straying over a dozen villages in a single expedition, taking a bath in a cow-puddle here, a drink from a hill tarn there; a day-to-day existence. He never once thought of returning to his old haunts or cliff or spinney, though once or twice he recalled familiar landmarks as he roamed the moors. All that had been blotted out in the gun's roar, and in its place a wilder aversion of human beings had been stamped in: for the rest of his life his nerves would bear their brand.

But it was not this alone that had unsettled him. In the early mornings there was fog and every leaf was crinkled with hoar sparklets. Sometimes he awakened to find his feathers crisped with frost, and when he set out hunting every mole-hill seemed deserted, not so much as a beetle stirring. Every day he had to travel further afield, work harder than ever before. As the year declined the light grew poorer, the sun withdrew into a wan sky, making his task still more difficult. His spirit constricted as the days grew shorter. All the dazzling freedom of his summer-time was clouded: even his hovering now had a lost, disconsolate air,—his wanderings were those of a lost soul.

He had no need of any past experience to tell him what

this restlessness, this endless dissatisfaction meant. He could feel its symptoms in his blood. He could read its diagnosis in the changed sky, in the voices of strange birds. The fields were empty.

All day he had struggled to make a living in that gale, fighting his way into it valiantly until every inch of him ached—and he had failed. It tossed him contemptuously among the storm of russet leaves as if he were of no more account than they. It tried to fling him to the ground, shatter the life out of him. It came at him sideways like an unexpected wave. Knocked him head over heels. When he breasted the rising ploughland (so low that his expectant feet trailed almost in the furrows) it held up its great fist in his face to drive him back. Worst of all, it came blustering at him from behind, plucking at all his feathers, dishevelling him and chilling his whole body. For all his pains he had got nothing.

Towards evening he took refuge on a telegraph-pole,—the first he had perched on since his early days in the river meadows. It was the likeliest place he could find, for all the trees groaned as they swung in the wind, their branches streaming like hair. He set his face towards its fury and did his best to settle in comfort. Somehow the day's wildness had left him feeling more uneasy than ever: all the time there was a dumb craving inside him quite distinct from hunger.

Beyond the low line of distant hills a wintry sunset spread out its golden shield, cold fire reflected through the firmament in various shades of fading pink. Above that halo of intense brilliance the roof of the sky was scalloped with crimson cloudlets, while from its centre smoky wisps splayed fanwise up,—streamers of smoky darkness that probed and strayed across the heavens. A luminous screen of gorgeous hieroglyphics. In the reflection of it Klee's feathers were burnished to shining bronze. The hills looked cold, ash-blue and dark against the horizon. This windstorm would last for days, he knew.

As he huddled against the sheltering wood he heard the strange cries of lapwings settling down for the night in their furrows, hysterical clatter of blackbirds in the hedge-row, going to roost. He saw the last wind-sprawling rooks and jackdaws go struggling homewards together, their ranks more untidy and disorganized than ever, though most of the wiser birds had come down to ground level and laboured along, looking almost like cockroaches in the distance. But even for these dodgers there were hedges to top, and when they tried to rise, the maddened air took them by the throat and pitched them back, all of a heap, cawing in protest. As if by contrast a pack of golden-plovers swished resolutely by, whistling softly as they mingled into the twilight. Arrow-winged sprinters. He envied them.

A crowd of Army lorries came rumbling down the road and though he was not in any way daunted by moving monsters of that kind he had an idea that somehow or other they were connected with men: accordingly he avoided them. Besides, he had still to find some place for his night's lodging. He could not, like these chiming buntings, creep into hedgebottom or make himself snug in any bankside cranny.

Releasing his hold, he allowed himself to be caught up into the towering sky, slashed now with silver rain from the bellying cloud into which he was ascending. The fields, the trees were swept under him like a moving carpet. As he rose, several flocks of smaller birds flew across his sky-path, all travelling in the same direction, wind slightly abaft their course and calling at regular intervals. The wind must have shifted a little . . . he gave up trying to force a way against it and followed these night-travellers voyaging into the unknown. Let the wind become his ally, not his master: he too could enjoy adventure, a journey. Leaving the cloud behind, he came through and out into a clear and tingling light, saw the first stars ahead, saw the hurrying flocks beneath him again, still speeding.

He could tell by the steady orderliness of their progress that they had already come a great distance: foreigners, —uttering a harsh unknown language.

Chak. Chakchak!, the fieldfares cried as they saw the hawk pursue them overhead, but they kept their course without wavering. After a time, however, leaders detached themselves from the hurrying crowds and came up to challenge him with angry shouts. Grey vikings,—their boldness reminded him of the stormy missel-thrushes that had mobbed him in the summer, but he ignored their clamorous company, forged ahead and presently saw them dropping down to rejoin their fellows.

Night now, and still he sped on. He took no thought of where his venture was leading him nor the nature of his journey's-end. It was enough that he was going. Already he was feeling easier for it, as if that inner craving were being satisfied, that tension released in the night's spaciousness. When he looked again the land had disappeared. In its place was a darker waste of waters, unmarked by hedge or lane, patterned only with flecks of white: but this, new as it was, did not seem dangerous or strange, and on he flew. He was his own compass and lodestar.

After two hours or more the wind changed again, blew more abeam and began to fall away a little. He came down and presently saw another group of dark forms winging beneath him close to the water, a chevron of unknown nightfarers. They were quite plain silhouetted against the waves' dull phosphorescence: like him they steered patiently towards the black wall of the South-West, sustained by an unspoken faith in the undiscovered future. It was now dead calm and for some time he kept station directly above them; but gradually the wind returned, veered round to for'ard, reducing his speed considerably, so that he, too, was forced down to sea level. In doing so he lost them.

Nothing now but a vast darkness, the lost murmur of wave crests. During the brief calm he had been able to see the endless sea-plain stretching to its black horizons, the shy moonshine ruling the world's rim, a shimmer in the luring distance: but now there was no distance, nothing with which to measure his progress, only the ceaseless effort of wings that were beginning to be weary. No star, no moon now. Nothing. Even Klee's eyes could not pierce the night's camera obscura, the murk.

Presently it began to snow, a few wet drops at first, then a thickening mush of flakes smothering his eyes, then a blizzard driving at him headlong. Try as he might, he could not face it and was compelled to alter course to avoid its pitiless onslaught.

For the first time his mind misgave him a little. He flew round, lost, trying to find a way out of that shroud of deadly bitterness. Lost, lost, calling out in solitary distress to the unanswering silence, while the settling flakes deadened his feathers and slowly weighed him down. Alone and lost.

But at last he came through, and out into a steelblue, starbright night again. He was too tired to shake his sodden shoulders and toiled on slowly into the icy, quivering blast. A faint hint of grey smudged the horizon behind him, but he made on towards the louring west. For there, whether on sea or sky he knew not, was a fixed point of yellow winking light, constant; glimmer beckoning him on through the endless tunnel of the dark. Not a star, surely. With his last strength he urged himself towards it, no longer tacking and veering, but with a crow's deliberation.

A great shape rearing and jolting in the water. A light that revolved, red, yellow and red,—a bell that jangled ceaselessly: but a resting place however heaving. Afraid of the noise and the light, Klee circled the buoy twice for all his weariness. Then without further precautions he settled on the inviting crossbar of iron. Let the bell boom, the lantern clank as it turned; let the waves snatch and smash, the whole structure shudder and spin,—he was beyond all caring. Without so much as a hitch of his wings he buried his face and slept.

Not long, however. He was not the only traveller to be attracted by that light. The darkness was suddenly alive with questioning bird-calls, needle points of sound that came and went in the gusty night as the little migrants approached, still fearing that strange brilliance yet unable to resist its hypnotic attraction. Soon they were clustering all round him thick as snowflakes—and not much bigger—crowding the rails, dropping off and trying to gain a secure place elsewhere, a flurry of midgets. Goldcrests. One of them even tried to settle on Klee's head and would have done so had he not moved. For long the night was full of their sibilance, but there were not places for more than a few, however tightly they packed themselves, and after a time the others were blown sidelong into nothingness. There was peace again,—except for the ceaseless jangling of the bell, the roar of wind and the sea surge.

Strange bedfellows, so thickly crowding, that he could feel the warmth of their tiny bodies pulsing at each side of him. If he had wished he might have picked them up and swallowed them at a gulp one by one: instead, he merely sat in their midst and watched. Once a great seabird showed a moment in the lantern's turning beam a momentary vision of ghost-white shearing the wave tops, leaving a wild cry behind it as it disappeared. Once a herd of swans went whooping by. . . .

He must have dozed. The sky was greying now, the horizon brightening into palest egg-shell greens. The goldcrests had gone. In their place was the lean humped figure of a greybacked crow, fast asleep. There was a light breeze blowing from the east and the freshening day gave promise of clearness. He was off again.

He flew, not towards the dawn, but away from it, still making towards the far South-West, as if pursuing the retreating night. Out there the massive sky was piled high with threatening clouds, but he knew that somewhere beyond it lay his destination, that his voyage was nearing its end. He could feel the gentler land air coming to greet him, the soft South.

Nor was he quite alone. Beneath him was a long phalanx of rust-red migrants heading in the same direction, —Woodcocks. They flew in slow, owlish fashion, so close to the surface that they barely topped the breakers, the leader occasionally falling back to give place to another bird so that the formation was continually changing. He could see their long bills pointing rigidly in front of them.

They were tired, tired. As he followed, a hundred feet above, he saw a straggler caught by a rearing arm of the surf: for an instant it lay outspread in the green trough, fluttering, then the next wave sucked it under for ever.

The others headed on, unseeing, unknowing. And at last the low land came up out of the ocean ahead of him, a silver edge to the surly horizon which gradually resolved itself into a gleaming mudflat, a low flat shore ridged with dunes, a bleak saltmarsh beyond. Before coming to landfall he let the off-shore breezes take him higher, saw the intricate windings of the coast far down, framed all the way with breakers, saw the new sunlight dappling the inland fields, the green sweetness of woods. He saw the slow woodcocks struggle across the angry maelstrom of reef-broken surf (a rock-pedestalled cormorant snaking its neck as they passed him), and as they went hurrying across the dazzling beach to pitch to rest in the sheltering dunes, he followed. The long night was done and though daylight had brought with it new readiness for action, he too was glad enough to fold his wings and seek the comfort and refuge of the quiet earth. He had come through. That was enough. His adventure was over.

Or was it? . . . Though he tried to make himself comfortable in one of the marram hollows he could not succeed in settling. The gritted sand found ways of penetrating his feathers, causing him to shift about all the time, though he was too far gone to summon up interest enough to preen himself thoroughly. All his plumage was in disarray, stiff and clogged with salt,—he would not be right again until he had found some place for a bath. Now that it was all over he suddenly realized too, that he was ravenous (—what creature can rest on a nagging stomach?), and the realization brought with it alertness, a fierce thirst for blood. Nor could he reconcile himself to a ground roost, least of all in daylight. Each time his eyeskin rolled away he saw marauding crows reconnoitring overhead, on the prowl,—and thought of Ronka. It was too dangerous.

He stood up, shook himself half-heartedly and set off to find what he could. For a time he quartered the dunes hopefully, but not for long, for the whole stretch seemed a lifeless desert apart from an occasional finch. For want of anything better he turned his attention to the sea-weed refuse heaped along the tide-mark, scattering clouds of white-winged snow buntings in front of him as he beat along. Their bell-notes tinkled in the wintry air, but he disregarded them and the gulls that came flying to greet him with harsh cries,—kept his head down, bent on his own business.

He had not gone far before he spotted the remains of a dead bird, strewn on the sand: but when he turned the battered relic over there was not even a picking on it,—the crows had been there beforehand. Only its wings and its dried skull remained to hold it together, the body had been scooped clean and hollow, so hollow, indeed, that even as he touched it the wind took it and began to roll it lightly along the sand. Once again his luck held, however; a little further, and he found a dead scoter still wet from the receding tide, its eyes still bright and bulbous. Though it was too big for him to pluck in the ordinary way he tore what he could from the great mound of flesh,—acrid, but wholesome enough,—and would have eaten far more had not his attention been attracted by a cry overhead.

Krarrr!

He looked up sharply. There, sure enough, circled a jealous crow, shouting for the whole neighbourhood to come and share his discovery.

Krarrr! he craked, too nervous to come down and challenge Klee unaided, yet outraged at the very sight of this trespasser who had somehow managed to forestall him at his own game. In a minute there were five more of them, and as they alighted, forming a ring, strutting and closing in upon him with a confident insolence which there was no mistaking, he took a last hasty pull at the red entrail strings and beat a retreat. Had he not been disturbed like this he would have stayed and stuffed until his crop was hard as a cricket-ball; still he had had enough to content him for the time being. Let the ghouls finish what he had begun. He left the sea behind him, and gliding effortlessly, began a lazy inspection of the tawny saltings, an immeasurable carpet of dead sea-lavender intersected by winding mudways that went winding, dark or silvery, towards the distant mainland. In the middle of one of the wider creeks there was a tall post sticking out of the glassy water, the very thing he had been looking for, and happily untenanted. A heron, fishing by itself near the bank, raised and stiffened its neck pole to full height, eyeing him with suspicion as he composed himself; then when it was satisfied, resumed its gawky wading in the shallows.

Klee spent the rest of that day there, quietly taking in the details of his new surroundings.

9

ALL through that winter Klee lived pleasantly enough, the grey marshland his headquarters. He made no effort to penetrate far into the interior, for there was everything he needed here—the first fields beyond the sea-wall were swarming with the fattest voles he had seen anywhere. In the early mornings and late afternoons he competed for these with the slow short-eared-owls: they roosted in the sandhills but were sailing abroad at all hours, even at midday. He never ventured afield at any time without meeting at least one of these grave hunters. Some days they would cross and re-cross his path a dozen times, turning their round faces and blinking their mild, dark eyes at him as they glided past. They knew, better than he did himself, which were the most populous corners and where a quick kill was likeliest to be made at any given moment,—useful knowledge, this, for the voles were for ever shifting their grounds. Klee learned a good deal from those owls, nor despite their superior size did they seem to regard his presence as an interference in any way, —probably because his methods were so different from their own. They flew noiselessly and apparently aimlessly, a few diffident wing beats and then a long glide on upraised wings, barely skimming the ground, suddenly turning and flopping loosely on top of their prey the moment it stirred. He preferred to work from a great height, watch the creature moving until he was sure of it, then drop down in easy gradual stages with a last exulting swoop. Neither method was invariably successful, of course, but in their different ways each was equally effective.

As far as food was concerned the level saltings were not

much good for anything, though he was not above sampling an occasional red-worm or a stranded shell-fish; still, he spent the greater part of his time there. He felt at home in the open spaciousness of the marshland, and its numerous look-outs made it a fit place for any hawk. Nor was he alone in thinking this. There was little Skild the merlin, as true-blooded a falcon as Hek himself, though scarcely bigger than a blackbird: to see him fly down a lark, doubling and twisting on his lightning switchback, carrying it off screaming in mid-air, was enough to rouse the admiration of every flying thing. There were other kestrels, too,—usually he saw them hovering in the distance,—but they were always busy with their own affairs, and he certainly felt no inclination whatever to start any closer acquaintance. He had his own life to lead, and they had theirs. One hawk was enough in the field, a second would only have been a hindrance. His own company was happiness enough. Had it ever been otherwise?

Of all the hawks of the marsh, however, it was Skandur the great hen-harrier who had the most obvious claims to distinction. Not that there was anything particularly distinguished in his mode of hunting, for that was always a slow and tedious business (pitiful to watch), but he covered the ground with a masterful lordliness which was impressive if nothing more. The whole of his upper-parts was pallid grey, the colour of Klee's tail, which looked well, but it was his length and lightness, the airy grace of his great wings, which set him apart from other hawks: an aristocrat of aristocrats. He was never known to hurry, for he moved at his own sweet will,—slothfully almost,—yet as light as a butterfly, flaunting his indifferent pinions and then holding them out while he glided fifty, sixty, a hundred yards. He was the terror of all the smaller birds. The first sight of him skimming the feathery reed-beds was enough to send whole armies of starlings whirring up in confusion, set the redshank sentinels fluting their warnings. On the mere the black coots fled splashing into the reeds, the sleeping wild ducks shot up their bottle-green necks and went whistling up. In the creeks the herons barked, looked up from their fishing and stood stiff until he had passed over. For a time the whole sky would be a broidery of interweaving birds, crowding and racing excitedly . . . and all for nothing. They had not learned, as Klee had, that Skandur, for all his impressiveness, was nothing more than an incapable humbug, a picker-up of offal and broken-winged birds. The sheer nimbleness of Skild's dexterity might be enviable in its matchlessness, but the way this false Skandur cleared the deck filled him with faint jealousy, even though it was none of his business.

Every time the harrier passed that way,—and this was by no means every day, for Skandur ranged over an immense territory,—it was Klee's habit to go for him, throw his sham dignity into confusion. He would even leave off in the midst of his preening to sally forth to the attack,—playful at first, of course, though he got in many a shrewd thrust when the opportunity presented itself. He liked best of all to cut downwind upon the harrier, just as it was at the end of one of its long glides, disconcerting it by the very accuracy of his determination, compelling it to roll or loop, or even to shout aloud in fear. When it came to the push, Skandur's air-skill was not to be despised, however; at the last moment he could whip up a sudden burst of speed, twist, double in a sudden menacing turn as lithe as the whiplash of a pinned grass-snake,—and though he was not easily roused he had his sudden nasty moods; so Klee was careful not to provoke him further than was necessary. Sometimes the pair of them would compete in these mock-battles, neat hawk and flaunting harrier, ascending higher and higher as they tilted, soaring.

Then there were the crows, grey-backs most of them from the far North, murderous brutes, every one, though here they did not try to persecute him much, for every bird came and went about this open seaboard without any thought of private punctilios or privileges. Every day he came upon their leavings,—a woodcock bludgeoned to death as it slept in the sandhills, a lame gull whose execution they had gleefully undertaken (—and how it shrieked as they dug in their blunt beaks!),—the weaklings, starvelings, the weary or unwary, the accident cases, all were fair game to the laughterless crows. When they were gone he was not averse to trying his luck with their leavings, but it was not often that they left much, usually not enough for a picking.

Of other birds he took little notice and no heed. The herons were his silent bodyguard for many an hour while he took his afternoon naps, and the redshanks were useful too,—though not so reliable, for there was always a touch of hysteria in their outcries,—too often they were false alarms. Some days they were a nuisance, in fact, squealing all round him as he sat there waiting for the next pellet of fur to disgorge itself.

At low tide the mudflats crawled with hundreds upon hundreds of little dunlin, mouse-like birds that never for a moment looked up from their feeding and never stopped running. All the time their twinkling black legs nimbled hither and thither over the shining surface of ooze . . . so mice-like that for weeks he could not help cocking his head down and gripping the post tighter in act to plunge—only relaxing when he realized his error. Still, the similarity was so marked that even now he could scarcely prevent himself eyeing them hungrily. But they were birds. Since his spinney days he never attempted to strike down anything feathered, though he had had more than one opportunity. It was not in his nature. Of course, if he lighted on one already dead, that was another matter altogether. . . .

So the winter slowly wore itself away, every day adding new point to his existence, each strenuous incident sharpening his wits, until he became the complete hunter. Grey days, pearly days, days of storm when all he could do was huddle in the dunes, listen to the wet wind stirring wirily in the marrams, days all adazzle from dawn to sundown when his old joy returned and he killed and killed again for sheer pleasure. Carefree.

And gradually he became aware of a change. In February there was a whole fortnight of clear days, a new softness in the clouds, a clearness in the air,—as though the year's eye were quietly beginning to open again after its long sleep. He could feel the change stirring in everything,—in the firmer touch of the sun, in the sharper tang of mouse-blood, a new silkiness in mole's felt,—most of all in the brighter gloss of his own feathers.

His feathers. As the days lengthened and lightened they became his increasing delight: he could scarcely leave them alone. The preening-ritual now became a craze. He had always been regular in his habits, of course, but never before had he spent so much time attending to his toilet. He fairly worried the old frayed feathers, plucked at the hollow quills to loosen them and hasten their moulting,—to such an extent that for a time his flight was seriously affected by their loss. He was almost conscious of the proud strength of the new ones, firm beneath his skin. Certainly he was aware of a difference in his outward appearance, an improvement. . . . His head, from a nondescript brown, had silvered to lightest grey; his barred mantle had given place to gold specked over with spots of jet. The bristles about his mouth stiffened as they lengthened; his moustache grew blacker and more pronounced than before, and the dinginess of his tail ends (hitherto a detail which had always left him dissatisfied) now assumed twelve tips of purest white. Best of all, however, was the heightened yellow of his legs, the deeper blue of his bill, the orange fleshiness of the skin which encased it and his eyes,—these showed he was no longer a youngster but a full-grown brave,—someone to be reckoned with. They gave him new confidence. His whole frame thrilled with a new exhilaration: and though for three whole weeks he spent most of his time just sitting about, he was only waiting for the good time that he knew must be coming. Often as he sat there on the post he was filled, flooded through and through, with unutterable joy—it threw him up in the air, quivering, a wild rippling in this throat. These outbursts grew more frequent as the spring drew nearer, came on him unawares. He was liable to break out at any time into these unpremeditated rhapsodies: and without such outlets sheer gladness would have stifled him. Never before had he been so irrepressibly vocal.

And all shaping towards some purpose yet unknown.

The tide was fuller than usual that morning, quietly gurgling around the barnacled post until it all but touched Klee's tail,—an oily mirror of blue. A deep silence brooded over the saltings, wakened only by the cry of a wandering gull. A kingfisher sped past, a blue sparkler —almost touching him—and as he turned his face to watch where it settled another flashed in his eyes. Only his movement prevented its perching on the post beside him; but it shot away up-creek without so much as swerving, piping shrilly as it chased its mate. Presently the two of them returned, one speeding close behind the other, both twisting and piping in great excitement, patins of turquoise and fire-opal speeding. Creatures possessed!—spring-fevered imps.

At times from the thronged bivouacs of the curlews there

would rise an unrestrained mad song as one individual after another found the growing tension too much for it to bear ; and then the whole drowsy flock would rub shoulders uneasily as though something had disturbed their fitful dreams. All through the winter they had spent the high-water hours in that islet sanctuary, packing it to the edges, but recently their ranks had thinned: nowadays they came straggling in in ones and twos, not in a close company as in the frosty season. At the first signs of the ebb, before the mud in the creek had had time to uncover more than an inch or two, they were gone again to their remote feeding places on the ooze-flats,—and there the delirium of their gladness knew no bounds: the distant foreshore was often all a-ripple with their cries.

Thoughts were straying, ties were loosening, daylight lengthening. Skandur was gone, and he had not seen Skild for days. Larks trilled now, unmolested, startled up from the sea-lavender, white flashes in their tails, quivered and burst forth into sudden frenzies of impassioned utterance. There was a new jerkiness in their mountings, and, once up, they could scarcely leave off running their little sky-rings. Even the white shelducks were not unmoved. Like the curlew's, it had been their custom to spend their quiet hours here in this safe retreat, a sleeping flotilla on the innermost waters of the creek. They used the islet as their windscreen in all weathers, the curlews as their watchdogs: and when the latter made their departure they divided their time between dozing and ablution. Sometimes they grunted at each other as they splashed themselves and beat their pied wings in the water, but for the most part they were heavy, stodgy creatures, phlegmatic in everything. Their only interest was to go a-paddling, waggle their red-knobbed bills in the slime, sifting the brine for crayfish or for weed, slobbering their food.

This morning, however, the whole of that shining flock

seemed to be on edge, afflicted by some undercurrent of suppressed excitement. The shelducks had all become strangely garrulous. And quarrelsome. The drakes stood up to their full height, showing off the handsome sheen of their dark viridian heads, swelling out their burnished bosoms, growling: then they began a ceremonious bowing, sawing the air with their beaks, breaking off in the middle of it all to dash at each other with necks outstretched. There was more show than spirit in these attacks, more noise than menace; a brief scuffle and one or other of the combatants retreated—whereat the victor, encouraged, would immediately dash at some other inoffensive drake. A crazy business. Meanwhile the demure females went on with their preening or bathing, seeming to take no notice of all this tomfoolery. But from time to time one of them would stretch her neck and take the air, crooning a mild invitation for her lords to follow; and follow they did, one, two, or even three of them craning their necks to catch her up and whistling softly as they flew. And what a mazy dance she led these suitors of hers!—trailing them after her as though they had been tied by some thread to her tail. Round and round she wandered, now slowing down to let them overtake her, then giving them the side-slip, while they in their breakneck haste tried to get in spiteful digs at one another. Usually it all ended in nothing,—the trios rejoined the main party on the water, coming in with a rush and splash, then forgetting all about it: but occasionally these love-flights ended in a choice being made and the pair would not return.

By imperceptible degrees the winter flocks were disintegrating; they melted and scattered as quickly as frost crystals now did under the morning sun. The night too, was no longer a dead pall only, but a skyway loud with its traffic of eager wings.

A bubble came wobbling up from the depths, burst with

a plop a few feet away. Through the green translucence Klee saw the shadowy fishes wavering their frail fins, the long wreaths of sea foliage waving underwater : and knew by their motions, by the yeast-froth creaming and eddying on the surface, that the tide had already turned.

Kee—kee . . . kreeee . . .

He bent his head to scratch and whinnied at his own face in the water. In that same instant his whistle was repeated from the sky overhead, an echo with a strange appeal. He looked up. There, careening in a wide arc, was another kestrel, a newcomer, someone whom he had not seen before, not even at a distance. A lady.

At other times Klee might have ignored the presence of this stranger,—when the mood was on him he might even have resented it,—but there was something compelling in the way she thus saluted him. Not that he had any scruples about attacking females,—it was just that there was something attractive about the easy way she carried herself into the wind, a feminine grace. . . . A beauty indeed. . . .

And a coquette, too, apparently. No sooner had Klee slid into the air, almost breasting the water as he dipped away from the post, than she drew off, silent now,—and though he called to her anxiously as he hurried upwind, there was no reply. He could see her getting higher and further off as he rose and called again, his voice full of tender pleading.

Keee . . . kee.

He did not know why he should follow her like this, nor why he should be so suddenly anxious to overtake her, —but he followed, calling after her at intervals. She was for ever swinging her head into the wind, lifting her wings so that the light shone on her streaky flanks, allowing it to carry her effortlessly down the endless seaboard. A wanderer, a gipsy, fancy free,—she led him on. Together they left Klee's winter ground fading behind them under the blanket of afternoon mist, traversed an unfamiliar length of rocky coast, a smudgy town, and came in the purple evening to a winding estuary where at last she paused, spiralling above the umber smoke-plume of a steamer. Klee circled with her, possessed with a quiet gladness, proud to show off his airskill in her company, —and on again she flew . . . whither he neither knew nor cared.

That night the two of them roosted together in the strange branches of a lonely tree.

10

THOUGH it would not be true to say that Klee's courtship had already begun, it is a fact that from that day forth Frikka and he became more or less inseparable companions, never losing sight of each other for any length of time without feeling themselves at a loss. They still went their own separate ways when hunting, but there was an unspoken understanding between the two which somehow resulted in an unfailing rendezvous each afternoon and evening, and though she gave no real sign of encouraging his attentions (—it was always a case of his seeking *her*, rather than the reverse), he knew that she did more than just tolerate them.

The weather had taken a change for the worse again, dark squalls and fitful gusts from the sea, and for a few days they took up residence on the fringes of a forested countryside, a warm, sheltered valley not many miles inland. For his own part Klee would have been content to stay there, for food was plentiful,—every glade had its mole-run and shrew colony,—but Frikka, he knew, was restless still, fretful and dissatisfied; and though nothing had occurred to link them inseparably, he was now to all intents and purposes under orders from her. Where she went he followed. Towards evening when she sat preening on the topmost tuft of a gaunt fir tree he would fly playfully around, showing off in a vague sort of way, hoping to please her. First he would rush past her, such a whuff of wings that she was compelled to lift her head to watch him, after which he would go boring up with clean, decisive pinion strokes, then turn and come planing smoothly back in a long slanting glide. For a moment or two he would sail around her tree, a dreamy, moth-like motion: then with a sharp cry he would clap his wings and repeat the process in another direction. Sometimes as he circled he called out to her wistfully, peevishly almost, for he could see her there still busy preening or even tucking her head in to go to sleep, taking not the slightest notice of his gallantries. There was no response. If she continued like this,—refused to let herself be interested,—he had other means of forcing himself upon her. Instead of planing down on her with motionless wings he would stoop headlong from the apex of his flight, dash on her suddenly in a steep dive, almost as if threatening to impale himself on the upspiking branch. Then when it seemed almost certain that he would (—and more than once his breast grazed hers as he turned),—he twisted vertically up, shouting his excitement. But even this display of warrior-like determination had only a momentary effect: she merely flinched, shifted her position an inch or so, and resumed her feathering. Klee kept it up for hours until he was quite worn out or lost interest. Then he, too, came in and settled for the night in the bare branches, either on the dead bough, edging diffidently alongside her . . . as near as he dared, —or by himself in the lower part of the tree.

As the days passed, Frikka grew ever more restless and sensitive, her moods fickle, shot through with passionate spasms. He could never be quite sure how he stood with her now at any given moment: sometimes when he tried his innocent games on her she turned on him savagely, drove him off, puzzled and disappointed. He could never understand what he had done to upset her so violently, —for their relationship had so far been quite free from quarrels or problems of any kind. He was left at an utter loss and flew round at a distance, aimless, bewildered, calling pathetically to the unfeeling emptiness of skyscape.

For three weeks wild March frowned and blustered about

the woods, then relented and showed a mild and smiling face again. The sing-song voices of the first chiffchaffs came stealing through the empty trees, delicate little birds with olive backs and sulphur-coloured eyebrows,—they crept about the higher branches so preoccupied with their search for early insects that they never once noticed Klee sitting there, alone and half disconsolate. From morn till night the sky was full of heron trails, the great birds constantly trafficking to and from their traditional nesting elms. Some of the nests already contained young birds,—he knew that from the way the hoary patriarchs and lean sentinels barked at him from the treetops as he passed over; the whole woodland rang loud with their hoarse and angry discordance. That morning Klee had killed a drowsy slow-worm rustling through the leaf-mould, not yet recovered from its winter sleep. The air was warm and still. As he sat there, wondering what to do next, he kept hearing the red bark as it curled and crackled in the quiet sun; every now and then a dry flake of it pealed off and twirled softly to the forest floor. When he lighted on ashen switches he could feel a new suppleness in their swaying boughs: the sycamores oozed gum at every pore.

Kee . . . kee-eekee . . .

He cocked his head and looked up. His own cry exactly! the same in voice and pitch, yet it was not he that uttered it. Overhead, hanging in the clear sky, was another kestrel, a male; and there beside him was Frikka, encouraging him with that old alluring ripple in her throat, obviously pleased to let him weave his spells about her. This newcomer had appeared from nowhere, out of the blue, and already his presence was more than acknowledged,—clearly the affair was fast becoming more than a flirtation. A rival!

Klee's wings twitched on his back at the sight of him. He stood upright, gripped the branch with bitter talons.

Then he snapped into action, went twisting among the tree tops and, tucking his legs in, began to mount sharply. For a time he climbed on a straight course as though quite regardless of the amorous pair that he was so rapidly leaving behind, then, when he had covered a quarter of a mile, he turned and made ready. There they were, still sailing and sporting. . . .

Frikka's new suitor never knew what hit him. Klee fell upon him from behind with such a concentrated viciousness that for a moment he lost control altogether and the two of them fell twenty feet or more, a clutching tangle of frantic wings. But it was Klee's claws that struck home; the other was the one to lose feathers. Borne down by the first speed and weight of that blind and thunderbolt blow, the newcomer made a lightning come-back, fought madly to free itself. At last he broke free, but it took him a minute to recover his scattered wits, and by that time Klee was rounding up Frikka, flying after her with an exulting battle-cry. She neither avoided nor invited his approach but went on with her easy spirallings as though nothing whatever had happened; silent still. She did, however, permit him to join her and soon he too was revelling, in carefree circles, tilting at her playfully, flying directly under her to let her see the smart colours on his back, then racing round with talons dropped to show his manliness. As he rose higher she even deigned to follow him, retracing the smooth arcs he had just cut; and at last he knew that he had won favour, for suddenly her throat swelled up and she uttered a long, delirious trill.

But it was only excitement at the approach of that hateful rival again. In his glory Klee had quite forgotten the third hawk, but now it came butting in again, breaking up the sky harmony of what might otherwise have been a promising situation. Neither male was in any position to attack, and, as if to complete the disenchantment Frikka now made off altogether, leaving the two of them to sort it out as best they could. The two of them at once pursued her, Klee bringing up the rear. Dipping and turning, they followed every little loop of her labyrinthine flight and still found opportunities for venting their personal grievances on each other. Though they were both mad with jealousy they were too preoccupied with their efforts to impress the elusive Frikka to do more than make threatening runs at each other, trying at the same time to gain and hold a favourable position near her. This mazy progress grew into a formal love parade, first one, then the other almost touching her tail with eager bill and all three of them rising and falling in an undulating chain, an unending arabesque.

In the end Klee could stand it no longer, this dancing attendance,—it was getting nowhere and the longer it went on the bolder and more intimate did the stranger become, flying so close above Frikka's back that he almost covered her, murmuring seductive nothings for her to hear. Once, twice she had spread her tail, glamorously. Klee was fast becoming little better than a looker-on. It made him mad. The next time they attempted it rage so blinded him that he hurled himself at them indiscriminately forcing them apart, bowled over the surprised Frikka and in the same moment went for the other with a dry rattle of quills. This time it was a fight to the finish. He made no attempt to climb, but kept up a rapid series of thrusts, in out, in out, chattering his savagery all the time. Overcome by the very resoluteness of his attack, the intruder had little chance of retaliating, not that it made any difference when he tried, —he preferred instead to drop away, hoping to escape the fury of such an onslaught and so gain time to adjust himself. But Klee would not let him alone, kept at him, hammering him ceaselessly. When he did manage to break clear Klee cut sideways and spurted in at him just as he was ruffling himself in mid-air, trying to compose himself a little: and this time he hooked his feet fairly and squarely into his back. He had to flap desperately to keep his balance, but he held on while he struck, needle-billed, again and again at his adversary's unprotected nape. The terrified hawk screamed aloud, somersaulted in desperation, but when they righted again, there was Klee still grimly fastened to his back, tearing whole lumps from it. Success blinded him, and when at last the other managed to wriggle over, get a claw at his belly, causing him to break apart, he still pursued him. But the other had had enough. The would-be suitor broke and fled, still squealing with pain and baffled petulance. Even then he was compelled to roll and flip sideways, for Klee was still not done with him, though all that remained was to speed his going. And go he did, the craven. Klee saw to it that no thought of return was left lurking in his defeated brain. He did not draw off until he saw that his enemy had suffered a complete rout, that his sole intention was to get away altogether; then with a last chitter of warning, he eased his wings and turned away in quest of Frikka.

He could still see her, a speck in the bright West. She had not moved from the scene of his first encounter and was still at her circlings . . . waiting . . . for him. The fact that she would have made herself equally welcome whichever of the two happened to return victorious from that duel made no difference,—such a grudging thought never occurred to him. She was waiting for *him*, and with masterful strokes he raced to claim her, filled with a buoyant exaltation.

Keekeekeekeekee! he called and she replied at once; and as he lorded it, girdling her round with narrow, imperious circles, he knew that she was won. Meekly she submitted herself to his unseen sway, answering his every skimming move with an easy elegance that somehow made her more dear. Planing, her whole body was spread supine for him to gaze on, all its feminine symmetry displayed . . . His Frikka ! The ardour of his longing rose inside him like a flame,—he canted and would have bestrode her there and then but he was awkward,—all he managed was a fleeting caress. But the very touch of her was electric. No sooner had he done it than she closed her wings and sank away beneath him, making straight down without a sound or pause, down through the trees, to abase herself on the bare earth . . . such a posture as he had not seen before.

For a moment he hung winnowing above her, nonplussed by her strange attitude, then he dropped down a few feet away and began walking towards her. His body was tense, tight with excitement. It made his steps stilted. As he came behind her Frikka was seized with a violent quivering fit. Her wings drooped fluttering at her side, her feet kept pawing the ground all the time as though she were in agony ; and her open tail, now spread to a barbaric semi-circle, was presented full in his nervous face. As he shuffled round, not knowing what to do, she pivoted slowly so that whichever way he went that tiara of more-than-peacock-gorgeous feathers was displayed full in his admiring eyes. As an invitation to love it was too overpowering : it made him bashful, ill at ease. In the end he felt he had to break out of that hot ecstatic trance or be consumed in it. He forced himself to turn away. The moment he turned his head she began ranting her disappointment at him, but he took no notice, merely began a languid rearranging of his feathers. He, too, could be indifferent when he pleased. Besides, now she was his, he could afford to be independent.

Left to herself, Frikka's transport of yearning did not immediately subside. With bowed head and tremulous wings she continued her passionate display, her tail waving up and down mechanically all the while, her feet still scrabbling to be satisfied. Then the mood passed. She relaxed, shook herself and joined Klee in his prosaic search for beetles.

From that moment there was never any doubt as to their future relationship. From now on it was Klee and Frikka . . . Frikka and Klee for ever.

In the days that followed they led a wandering life together, getting to know each other more closely, coming to understand one another's little idiosyncrasies, delighting in little tendernesses which grew ever freer and more intimate. For Klee they were elysian days, days of pure ravishment, skylinked with Frikka in the highest heavens. Every morning he presented her unfailingly with a shredded mouse, so unfailingly indeed that she grew lazy,—let him do her hunting for her. Far from resenting this, Klee esteemed it an honour and revelled in the execution of his double duties. And though she soon came to expect food from him he never consented to hand it over without performing a little ceremony. The moment he alighted on the bough beside her he bent his head forward, pressing the mouse in to his breast, and, drawing himself up to the full stretch of his legs, walked stiffly and primly towards her. If all went right she would bow her head likewise and come to meet him. In this attitude, their bodies rigid as rulers, they advanced head down until their foreheads met and rubbed together. This done he dropped his present at her feet and flew off, either in search of more or (this was more usual) to circle high above her, admiring and knowing that he was admired. Sometimes, however, she was hungry and attempted to snatch the food before the proper time; which had made him dash angrily at her on more than one occasion or even fly off altogether and leave her hungry. Such little tiffs, however, were fleeting. They were as momentary, as shallow and as meaningless as the lightest scurryings of a breeze on still lake-waters.

They had come again to a low seashore. He could tell

by the way Frikka's eyes strayed that she was only waiting for a favourable wind, and from the lurching drift of the clouds he knew that that would not be long. He too was waiting, eager . . . for what? There was a ripeness warm inside him, ready to burst, a fullness eager to break out at any moment into floods of ecstasy.

That morning as he swept in alongside his mate upon the bough he knew that their moment was come. Frikka made no attempt to seize the meat too hastily and at the warm touch of her brow on his he kindled. This time he did not fly off but hung behind her longingly while she stooped and bolted it hungrily. In the midst of her meal she was suddenly transfixed with another of her blind spasms. Her maiden limbs were a shimmer of passion, her whole body twisted and stiff, an arch of uncontrollable desire gaping to be satisfied. And Klee was ready this time for the lightning consummation, the last embrace. Love riddled him through and through.

Frikka was very lovely. . . .

That evening the pair of them set out across the northward ocean, travelling lightly with the assistance of a steady sou'westerly breeze. It was a warm spring night, the northern moon spreading a tinsel-glittering path in front of them as they flew. For company they had flock after flock of straggling lapwings, some high (the moonshine flickering silverly upon their underwings), some pressing close to the smooth sea (blacker than crows, these). Side by side, they flew in silence; without any sense of effort. Rapture at each other's presence sustained them both, and would have made light of any gale: theirs was the luck of lovers.

Long before morning they had crossed the dark barrier of coastline and settled themselves to slumber under the dusty rafters of a village belfry.

II

It was Klee's turn to feel dissatisfied. Frikka was obviously preparing to make a home in the inner chamber of the old church belfry, and though her word was law he could not help feeling a little uneasy at such a choice. The place got on his nerves. There were too many people passing through the graveyard below, bare faces staring up, voices,—and the heavy booming of the bell unsettled him. Then there were the jackdaws, filthy, untidy creatures,—if they were not flocking round to mob and taunt him as he sat on one of the warm spire crockets they were for ever cackling and clacking in their crowds as they flapped in and out of the open arches. The beams were thick with their disgusting ordure. His face wrinkled at the thought.

Somehow Frikka must have sensed his aversion,—perhaps it showed as a strangeness in his manner towards her,—for after the third day she forsook the old church altogether and began searching for some more suitable site in the open countryside.

First she tried the wooded cliffs where the river swung into a narrow winding gorge; and for a whole morning she flew up and down the dripping face of limestone crag, lighting on ledges, slipping off again to try further along, peering into possible crannies, scrabbling to gain a hold in the cavelets formed by the naked roots of precarious trees. Meantime Klee mounted guard overhead and watched her. He had only a vague idea of what she was after: in any case it was none of his business. For him it was merely a question of waiting, riding at anchor over the green waving tree-tops. For Frikka, on the contrary, it was becoming a matter of urgency: her time was getting short. Nook after nook she tried but none would do: they were either too exposed or the interiors were damp or there were signs that rats had been thereabouts recently. Each time she emerged, shook the loose soil from her back and tried elsewhere, and every time he saw her reappear the watchful Klee called to her to join him, to come disporting; but she took no notice.

It irked him, hanging about like this,—this waiting; he almost felt tempted to go off on his own accord,—but still he could not bring himself to leave her even for a moment. The fierce edge of his passion was already blunted a little,—though always liable to blaze up between them at any moment; but she was his mate, his Frikka, and he was still her faithful worshipper. He stayed. To and fro he glided against the face of the crag like a slow, wide-swinging pendulum.

Suddenly there were sounds of a scuffle; he heard Frikka's shout of alarm as she came arrowing out of a cave, with another kestrel worrying her, screaming at her tail. Before he could come to her assistance he was himself sharply challenged from above and a quick glance was all the warning he had of the attack which immediately followed. Unwittingly they had strayed into the nesting territory of another pair,—a mistake for which there is neither pardon nor excuse. There was no facing up to the outraged indignation of the rightful owners, no question of fighting back,—the only thing to do was to get out of it as quickly as possible, and this he did, casting his stout pride to the winds and fleeing precipitately.

He came up with Frikka again a mile or so downstream, and though that untoward incident was already dismissed from their minds, its fleeting ignominy erased, they did not immediately resume their search for a likely home but idled about for the rest of the day in a white orchardland. That evening Frikka busied herself again, Klee following her the while in puzzled fashion . . . and at last she found what she was looking for,—a hollow ash tree with an old jackdaw's nest hidden in a deep recess (on the ground beneath was the mouldering arm of the tree, still lying where the wind had torn it from its socket to make that hole). There were new sticks in the nest, indicating that its previous tenants had recently thought of rebuilding and then for some reason changed their minds, but its great advantages were its height and its sheltered position. A great beam covered and concealed the entrance, screening a sunken interior chamber from the rain and wind; and another point in its favour was the ample number of perches either for peering down into twilit interior or for having a quick look-round before entering in. Frikka at least thought it the very thing,—and that was that: as far as Klee was concerned anything would have been good enough.

He soon found, however, that it *did* concern him—and very directly too. That night Frikka roosted in the nest and when he tried to join her there she refused to have him near her, jabbed at him in temper and finally drove him out altogether. He spent an uncomfortable night, shifting from one foot to the other, blowing up his feathers every minute to keep out the cold,—alone on the edge of the broken bough outside.

In the morning she showed no signs of venturing forth from the darkness, and though he called to her again and again to come away she refused even to look up at him. He could see her lying full length in the cupped hollow, fistling about all the time, rubbing her breast in to flatten it, moving a twig or pulling out a tuft of horsehair from the lining,—as though she would never be able to arrange it to suit her fancy. For a little while she would lie still, her head bolt upright and staring, not a feather stirring, but then the neurotic itch returned and the crackling of sticks, the fidgetings, began all over again. She had been like this all night.

Finding that he had no power to tempt her out, Klee flew off by himself, returning at once with a young rat (its tail still squirming). Before flying in to the nest he alighted on the top of an isolated elm by the riverside and from that point of vantage took the precaution of surveying the whole neighbourhood.

From then on that elm was *his* tree. Frikka's,—the ash,—was across the water, two hundred yards in a crow-line: he could see the whitethroats fussing and effervescing in the chaffy nettles and willow-herb sedge which clustered tall and thick about its base: she had chosen better than she knew,—in a few weeks' time the tree would be unapproachable, defended on every side by an impenetrable tangle of weeds. The reed-fringed river surrounded the tree on three sides, and a quiet corner of the high-hedged orchard approached it on the fourth.

Everything seemed quiet enough, but he could not feel certain about it . . . he could not help being anxious about Frikka sitting there by herself all this time. . . .

At times men's distant voices came blustering through the apple trees and, though they grew no louder, remained hidden, he knew they were still lurking somewhere behind that wall of creaming blossom. He dropped the rat from his bill,—easier to hold it in his foot,—and waited.

Still no sign of Frikka.

As he sat, all kinds of irrelevant details caught his swivelling eye,—a red spider running on the lichen beside him, the moorhen which came stealing up from the water's edge, nodding its head and jerking its tail through the grass, the wet otter that came nosing over the bankside . . . (sign sure enough that all was well),—but through them all he maintained an unwinking focus on *the* tree. Now a missel thrush topped it, weathercock-wise, sang a few spirited notes; now a bevy of prattling goldfinches was seated in its branches. . . . Good enough!

Picking up the rat in his bill, Klee flew swiftly towards the nest, uttering his clear call-note once, twice, thrice in rapid succession. He swept straight in and landed with a metallic scrape of claws on the level branch above the hole.

Ki-kee!

And there sure enough was Frikka poking her head out expectantly and coming towards him to be fed. The presentation ceremony over, she quickly disposed of the meal and disappeared again into the aperture, leaving him to mount guard outside. Though she had added nothing of her own finding to the nest she seemed to be more at ease in it than before, rather more at home. By this time even Klee knew that an event was near, a crisis approaching . . . and it made him curious. Again and again he ventured along to peep in at her, sitting there so woodenly immobile, murmuring in his throat with wonder that she should be so still. Then he grew bored and left her to get on with it while he quartered the lush meadows in search of something to eat.

For three days it continued like this. On the fourth day Frikka was more like her old self. She consented to accompany him on his farings again, and when in sheer bravado he picked an uncovered leveret from its form and flew on without even checking his original swoop she chased after him, begging him to make her a present of it. But the game was too good for him to forfeit it so soon, and after so many days' sobriety he felt the need of a little fun, so he held it every so gently so that she might hear its continuous anguished caterwauling. But she drew off in spite of all his coaxing and would have returned to the nest in a huff, so that he had to humour her after all. Disappointed again, he had to double back and cut her off, dropping the dead leveret for her to catch: which she did easily enough though not with the old zest.

That afternoon Frikka laid her first egg. Afterwards she went hunting by herself, the first time for more than a week, and Klee remained behind long admiring this round and ruddy jewel with which the dead nest was now so miraculously graced. Even in her absence he did not dare to inspect it more closely; but now that something tangible had appeared he was more content to do his solitary sentry-go, stay passive for long stretches. He felt satisfied.

Frikka no longer remained quite so tied to the nest chamber. She did not begin to brood at once; indeed for two days she seemed almost carefree again and indulged with him in many an airy sporting, letting him fondle her in mid-air, twisting and pitching head to tail until the pair of them were quite weary. Then they would rest awhile together on the look-out elm, and Klee would display to her, depress his tail and droop his quivering wings and ruttle in his throat, whereat she was quite overcome with emotion . . . until that glorious feeling flared up again inside them both and their wild bodies surrendered themselves in a searing flash-point.

On the second evening there was a second egg, more nobly marked than the first, freckled all over as if with dried blood, very handsome. Next day Frikka began to brood in earnest and in the interminable period that followed (actually it was four long, long, long, long weeks), she remained shuttered in close confinement, never leaving her eggs for more than an hour at a time. It was not merely that she was patient,—the eggs were her whole life, and she gave herself up to them entirely. Every second day there was a secret addition to her precious cluster, until, a fortnight after the first appeared, she had no less than six of them tucked neatly under her,—a perfect tally. Towards the end of that period the only occasions on which she would think of leaving them were at mealtimes,—and then only for hasty snack, bolting her food in a minute or two and disappearing again.

As for Klee, he had all his work cut out now to provide for both of them, so that he had small time for anything other than hunting. In this, however, he was still fancy free, trying the meadows or greening cornland or upland pastures,—whichever pleased him or seemed most likely to bring a quick yield. Whatever it was, his first catch was always for Frikka: the moment he seized it, he towered a hundred feet and set a direct course for home,—or rather for the watch-tower on the elm. Invariably that was his first call. No matter how quiet things might seem,—and from a height he could usually form a pretty good idea of what was going on in the neighbourhood—he would never permit himself to for go this necessary precaution. There he waited, a minute or two, perhaps, if all was well,—an hour or more if his suspicions were aroused in any way. Once, when he saw a man pruning trees in the orchard, he waited a whole morning for the all-clear—and then got a sound scolding for his pains from the famished Frikka.

He had become more than ever attached to his elm. He even roosted in it: and when he was off duty,—which was not often,—he used to sit up aloft there and keep an eye on things from a safe distance. He was rather afraid of the nesting tree,—the atmosphere there was too oppressively dangerous. It was not often that he had to utter a warning, though sometimes bands of children came gathering sticks or men shouting the cows home, waving their arms and driving him almost frantic with apprehension: and when at last fear got the better of him and he flew off repeating his keen penetrating, alarm-note, Frikka still refused to budge. Nothing perturbed *her*. Her eggs were a magnet fastening her to the nest whatever happened. She heard and understood his cry, but what went on in the world outside was now no more than half real to her, very far away; and if a twinge of fear did manage to penetrate into her cave,—and more than once her eyes dilated and her heart swelled with it,—it had no power to overcome her. She remained constant, rooted in her nest: whereas Klee, hovering at a distance, suffered agonies of helpless anxiety until the intruders had moved elsewhere.

Fortunately there was no shortage of supplies, nor difficulty in maintaining them. Moles were everywhere busy excavating new tunnels,—just a matter of choosing the right time and waiting overhead for their blind snouts to poke through,—and he had discovered the most profitable of rabbit warrens. The foolish parents there were just leading forth their first batch of babies, and it was the easiest thing in the world to pick up one of these innocent, unsuspecting infants as it strayed too far from the burrow's mouth. The field mice, too, were breeding, and he saw to it that their numbers did not increase unduly. If he was lucky in the morning, and if all was as it should be in orchard and meadow, he might venture to keep company with Frikka, sitting on the torn arm of the tree and looking in at her. How satisfied and motherly proud she looked! He could see it in the brooding mildness in her eyes. And for a time he, too, knew contentment. Placid hours!

Most of the time she sat there like something stuffed, but every hour she would stand up and stretch her cramped wings, her stiff tail, or turn about, nosing the hot eggs together into more comfortable patterns beneath her. Sometimes she would jump up beside him and sit preening, for after sitting so hard and so long all her breast feathers were in deshabille. There were marks on her body, naked, deep holes wherein she had pressed the eggs so lovingly, and her tail feathers were all but ruined with wearing so long against the rough bark.

Very occasionally she would allow Klee to take a turn on

the nest himself, while she permitted herself the luxury of a jaunt for exercise or a bathe in the meadow stream. For sheer want of anything better to do he had even known himself to be bold enough to enter her chamber and try to push her off,—gently of course,—and once or twice he had succeeded in persuading her to leave with hints less forcible. It made a change. But he was not very good at it; and at first he could never quite manage to make himself comfortable, though he was always careful to lie very still. He had not Frikka's breadth of bosom, and however much he spread himself there was always one egg at least kept peeping through,—no matter how he arranged and rearranged them. Then, just when he was beginning to get the knack of it the zealous Frikka would make her whirlwind entry, with such an imperious glance that he had no choice but to betake himself off at once. Though she allowed him short spells alone with the eggs like this, she neither asked for nor expected his assistance, and it only needed a moment's tardiness,—a hint of hesitancy in his going,—for her to fly in a rage. When she came he went.

One morning in the middle of the third week Klee had his longest—and his last—turn at incubating. He had been out in the red-eyed dawn, trapping two dew-soaked moles in quick succession, both of which he had brought to the nest. The second he shared with his mate,—they ate it facing each other on their trysting-bough above the nest,—and he was just about to make for the elm top (as usual) when without either cry or sign she suddenly launched out and disappeared over the orchard tops. She would be away some time (at least the determined way she cleft the air in her abrupt departure suggested it), and Klee did not need any further encouragement; he was coming almost to enjoy this sitting on the eggs. There was comfort in their smooth, firm shapeliness; and to feel the slow interior warmth of them throbbing against his body was a pleasure he had not previously known. He crept in cautiously and settled himself.

As the sun worked round the day grew steadily warmer. Soon the inside of the nesting chamber was like an oven. (Frikka must have felt it coming,—hence her apparent neglect. In such conditions the eggs could safely be left to hatch themselves, and she knew it. Klee's labour of love was not really necessary.)

He was sitting in a curiously tense position, his wings folded tight on his back and his breast fluffed to its uttermost, his head bolt upright and facing inwards. The interior was cramped in the extreme. Sitting that way his beak was not more than an inch from the bare wood,—he could hear the tree lice clicking away at their work in its secret hollows, and from time to time grey beetles would peer cautiously from their circular tunnels or come clambering up his neck. Klee never stirred.

After a time he grew tired of sitting with his back to the light, so he stood up, shook himself vigorously and, putting down each foot with exaggerated care, he sank into position with his face towards the entrance. It meant sticking his tail up at a steep angle,—and even then it caught awkwardly in a cleft of the bark,—but apart from minor details like this it was altogether more comfortable and pleasing. That side was free from shadow, and he could bask in the hot brilliance.

There was no view,—only the sky and one or two swaying boughs, intersected above by a moving filigree of slenderest branches. When the first egg was laid the ash had been quite bare, ironbound, but now every arm and finger of the tree was weighted with tasselled bunches of seeds. Every day now the lean and glossy foliage provided thicker shade, a bright tent of leaves.

He sat there drowsing in a long forgetful dream, thinking nothing, fearing nothing, caring nothing—not even troubling to ask himself why Frikka had not yet returned. The intense heat made his mouth dry. In an effort to get more air he had to sit there with his beak wide open, gasping all the time as if in dire distress . . . but so flooded with quiet happiness that he was scarcely conscious of physical discomfort.

And there were diversions. Sometimes Tchatchekki the spotted woodpecker would come bouncing across from his orchard home to busy himself with his carpentry-work on the dead branch just above the nest. There he was now,—a dazzle of black and white with a flash of deepest crimson on his head and bright scarlet vent,—hunching his bony shoulders and sending the chips flying. Some of them dropped into the eyrie, and the sawdust came floating down on to Klee's motionless mantle. An alert fellow, Tchatchekki, his mood always staccato, but he had not noticed the hawk sitting there and came jerking backwards down, hammering as he came. For a moment he hung there as if nailed to the trunk, darting his wedge-head rapidly from side to side, then froze, statuesque as he saw a blue sparrow-hawk come sneaking round the hedge corner.

Tchik! he exploded, snapping his chisel bill in alarm : and flattened against the trunk.

Though he could not see the cause, Klee read fear in the woodpecker's tense stance, and at that cry he shifted a little, ready to bolt for it at the first sign of danger. But then the bird above him relaxed again, edged sideways round the bole and disappeared behind the bend. He could hear him scraping about on the bark still, and presently the whole tree was jarred by his intense drumming. Klee could feel the vibration of it in his body : the entire tree was shaken by its concentrated violence,—the very air reverberated with the dull resonance of those whirring blows.

Tchik-tchik!

Now the gay climber was backing into view again,

twisting his neck round, not looking where he was going. When he did look he got the fright of his life, for there, not two feet away, was a great gargoyle facing staring hideously at him,—Klee gaping. With a startled scream Tchat-chekki fled, horrified . . .

Afterwards things were very quiet for a time, though there were always the goings and comings of a pair of starlings to observe. It was not until he started to sit that Klee learned that the tree already had other occupants. From time to time he had, of course, seen starlings perching in its branches, glossy crooners that sat in rows chuckling to themselves and beating time to their own music with tremulous waving wings,—careless troubadours gifted only with shallowest voices but an endless store of tales to tell. Here in his spy-hole, however, he could see them squeezing in and out of their inconspicuous doorway, a mere crack in the tree-stem. Though at most times the first glimpse of a hawk would have sent them scattering the starlings took no notice whatever of Klee's (or Frikka's) continued presence there. For one thing, they were far too busy attending to the needs of their newly born babies, which kept up an endless susurrus, clamouring to be fed from earliest dawn to nightfall. Both parents slaved to satisfy them: every few minutes they came, bill-crammed with insects, shooting straight in despite the narrowness of the aperture. What a gabbling crescendo greeted them, too!—it kept Klee cocking an eye each time,—then out they flung again, sometimes carrying in their yellow bills a little bag of ordure which they dropped at a safe distance.

Then there were more casual visitors. A fat wood-pigeon used to come and sit there from time to time, crooning some pompous nonsense or other while he waited for a favourable moment in which to slip down to drink at the river's edge. A clatter of wings and he was gone. Thirsty fellows, pigeons. Or families of long-tailed tits came weaving through the branches, or linnets came to chant, or swallows twittering,—always something.

Hotter still, and hotter! Frikka had never been away so long as this before. He half rose and began to move the eggs, pushing them into a more compact clutch, something he had not attempted before. Then he tried a new position, not so full in the sun's eye, and lowered himself wearily on to them again.

There was something very curious about those eggs. He kept bending his head to peer beneath him, not knowing what to expect. Very curious indeed,—he could not make it out at all. Once again he stood up, rolled the foremost of the eggs over and bent an ear to the shell to listen. Sure enough, the sound came from inside. A steady rhythmic tapping. As he watched, very intent, he saw a tiny crack appear. A movement! Then the noise stopped, the egg became inert again.—but only for a moment. There it was again! Most curious. He could not rest for wonder at it. Every minute now he had to stand up to have a look, and when he tried to brood he kept shuffling uneasily, feeling that something was about to occur at any moment. The low sounds continued inside the egg—like the slow ticking of a hidden clock,—he could feel its soft insistence against his breast-bone.

A shadow flicked across the sun, and, with a low chatter to herald her approach, Frikka returned. For a brief moment she stood on the upper bough waiting to take over, and they changed places without further salutation. For a time Klee sat in the elm cooling himself and setting himself to rights. In the late evening he did a little prospecting in the meadows, but he did not return to the nest again that day.

The same night the first of their eyasses was born, a blind and woolly mite: and from that time forth Frikka gave him no further opportunities of dabbling in domestic affairs.

12

WITH the arrival of the young, Klee's mode of life underwent yet another change. A new cycle was begun. From now on it was hard work and nothing else, particularly in the early days, for Frikka still spent most of her time brooding the tender babes, and at first he had to provide for all seven of them. (One of the eggs remained obstinately lifeless, though she continued to sit upon it earnestly long after the last chick had forced an exit,—until at last she lost interest in it. For days it was rolled about in the nest, useless lumber : in the end she carried it off and dropped it in the river.)

All day and every day he ranged afield, nursing his strength and using all the skill and sky-mastery with which experience had endowed him. For Frikka or himself anything was good enough,—withered shrew or tough vole, nothing came amiss,—but for the youngsters it had to be mice or nothing. And mice were not so easily come at now that the meadow grass was so thick and tall. His new responsibilities made him bold : even the haymakers shouting or machine rattling and roaring in the field could not daunt him,—he winnowed and came still lower, throwing discretion to the winds. Rather face them and all their noisy terrors than return a minute late or empty-handed to be scolded by that termagant, Frikka. He *had* to make a catch at all costs.

Once he dared to raid a farmyard, catching up a yellow duckling and sending the hens all scattering in fright ; but when he came a second time he noted a difference, a shape that glinted on the feather-flecked greensward, and he sheered off, too suspicious to take the additional risk.

Usually he tried to get back every ten minutes,—bring something however small,—if he was away much longer his reception was apt to be a stormy one. This meant a drastic curtailment of his usual ranging methods: he had barely time to race clear of the nesting territory a hasty half mile before he had to begin thinking of making a catch. Though the orchard and the riverside were alive with creatures he left them severely alone: he would never, never consider killing anything so near to the nest. No matter how desperate the need, it was an understood thing that hunting should never begin until the eyrie was well out of sight.

Whatever it was, mouse, shrew or mole, it first had to be properly prepared, stripped of its fur and pulped in his talons so that it was ready for the impatient Frikka to dole out at once to the ravenous young. But this was the work of a moment,—he did not even allow himself time to bolt the unusable fragments,—and off he flew with it to his elm, then with a low whistle, announcing his arrival, to the nest. Or rather to the presentation platform just above it. As often as not she was there waiting for him, craning her neck out as he landed. Klee was still rather averse to handing over the goods immediately, but the ceremony between them was now perfunctory, and if the eyasses were particularly agitated she merely snatched the meat and left him bowing and scraping by himself.

Before feeding the young, Frikka always took the greatest care to ensure that the food was torn piecemeal, shredded to finest threads, and though their spotted orange throats leaped at her like flames, she never allowed the youngsters to hurry her. To each in turn she gave a ration, eating the indigestible portions and bony remnants herself. At the first scent of blood five flabby throats shot upright, five skinny mouths reached over towards her, and the whole family squealed in desperate need, as though they were already dying of starvation; but she refused to be flustered by their insistent clamour. She took her time. There were, in fact, occasions when Klee returned to find her still busy parcelling out his previous contribution: in which case he would hop on to the entrance perch and watch her at her housewifery. From the start she had been most particular in matters of cleanliness,—and if the lining *was* becoming fouled with white splashes at least there was no mark upon her feathers and the fledglings were spotless, radiant. She even troubled to fetch fresh sprigs of larch, removing them when they dried and bringing new ones, and these she arranged round the edges as decorations.

Klee would gladly have stayed an hour watching the heaving, hitching pile of youngsters,—their sudden upsurging hunger, gyrating heads,—but she could not bear to see him idle for a moment. His presence, besides, only made the young more restless and difficult to deal with. After each meal she liked to collect them together, huddled in an indiscriminate mass, and cover them all with her warm feathers. Very proud she looked when everyone was comfortable at last; matron contentment softening the ruthless savagery in her eyes, but if he were anywhere near, the eyasses would not lie down nor cease struggling.

Klee knew better than to outstay his welcome. If he forgot, or if he allowed himself to become *too* interested in what went on in the nest, he was soon sent about his own business. She had given him more than one sharp reminder.

For a fortnight he slaved as never before, until the pads of his toes were sore and cracked with much pouncing. Often he had no time for a bath: some days he was not even able to give himself a thorough preening, and, hastening to every quarter of the compass, he dealt indiscriminate slaughter wherever he went. In the late evenings when the last rooks went labouring to their wood he was still busy quartering the deserted fields for toads that came out in the dewy twilight: they were easily caught and made a tasty supper, quickly served, for the young. A few hours' fitful dozing, listening to the nightingale exploding in the orchard or barn owl's bloodcurdling cry, and he was up before the dawn, hoping for an early kill to give a good start to his new day.

The intense strain was beginning to have its effect: it was more than flesh and feather could bear. It made him nervous over trifles,—he did not make thirty, forty errands to and from the nest each day without his appearance suffering: he was shabby and knew it. There were now no more love interludes between Frikka and him. They both had their separate work to do, and there was no time for much else. Most of the time she treated him like a stranger.

It was not until the young began to show their first feathers that Frikka would consent to leave them and share the burdensome duty of providing for their family. The days were warmer now and the eyasses were growing vigorous and hardy: no longer did she need to spend a quarter of an hour selecting titbits for their delicate throats,—she simply tore the mouse in lumps, fur and all, and gave a portion to each, letting them deal with it as they wished. And an unruly, pushing family they were,—all except one, a frail and meek little individual, the last-born of the five. The others were always taking advantage of his weakness, his inoffensive nature, stealing his food and worrying him with their sharp bills, standing on him and pushing him under regardless of his pleading cries. Not once did Frikka intervene to chide these bullies: indeed if she flew in while an assault of this kind was in progress she would stand aside and watch the mauling with the greatest interest, almost approvingly. Let nature take its own course,—that was her philosophy; there was no place in the world for a hawk without spirit, a weakling. Better eliminated.

Next morning she unearthed the strangled little corpse from under the struggling, protesting pile which had overlain it during the night. Carrying it in her bill, she dumped it, like all the other refuse, in the river reeds.

Although she was now away from the nest for long and longer intervals Frikka nearly always contrived to be there when Klee returned. She was still most jealous of anything which came between her and her offspring, and though they were now quite capable of tackling a whole mouse unaided, she insisted that feeding them was a specialized job which only she could do properly. True enough when she fed them the young were almost orderly, each waiting its turn and receiving its appropriate share: whereas when Klee came in with food he did not even alight in the nest but dropped it in from above, cocked an eye at them squawling and fighting for it, and then flew off, leaving the whole eyrie in an uproar.

As Frikka took over more and more of the actual field-work, Klee's life gradually returned to normal. He was still regular with his contributions, but nothing like so frequent,—nor did he now have that sense of fateful urgency hurrying behind him all the time. He was quite prepared to let her do the lion's share of the work and spent whole hours keeping a look-out for her on the elm while she was away. If all was well when she returned he might fly out to greet her and escort her home,—or he might just give his low whistle to let her know everything was all right. . . . Klee was feeling rather casual these days, careless, good-for-nothing. Not that he had lost interest in the family,—far from it,—but Frikka was now quite capable of looking after them by herself. In fact she preferred it that way. In family affairs he was fast becoming a nonentity.

How long it would have been before Klee finally resigned his domestic duties, dissolved his partnership, must remain a matter for argument and conjecture, for no sooner had he begun to relapse into this lazy slackness than something untoward occurred, an incident which completely upset the rhythm and orderliness of his whole existence.

He had been out early as usual and, chancing to alight on a hayrick gable for a moment or two, had had the luck to catch a young rat which came prowling out from the straw underneath his very feet. It was a very heavy rat, and as it was far too much for him to eat at a single meal he decided to carry it as best he could and present it at the eyrie.

When he arrived, however, there was no sign of Frikka, which was most unusual considering the early hour. The eyasses, too, looked chilled and miserable, huddled anyhow in the nest, too weak apparently to want to lift their heads. Perhaps she had just fed them? . . . He dropped the rat in among them and flew off.

For the rest of the morning he thought no more about it.

The early afternoon he spent in the elm, preening himself, listening to the furtive titmice fussing about in the greenery beneath, the tree-creepers threading their way through crannies in the bark, the cheeky chaffinches spinking at him, all unseen. . . . For a whole hour he sat there expecting Frikka to appear. In the end the persuasive warmth tempted him to drowsiness and he dozed,—only the moving shutter of his milky eye-skin showing that he was still awake, watchful.

In the middle of this blank reverie he was suddenly aroused by penetrating cries from the eyrie. In a flash he was streaking across the river, calling a welcome to his returning mate; a welcome that dried in his throat, became a harsh stammer of horror, as he saw that the bird inside was not Frikka at all, but an ugly headed monster apparently in the very act of devouring the young. His glad homecoming was arrested in an instant: instead of entering confidently he was transfixed in mid-air, nonplussed and terror stricken, his wings a whir of panic, his throat an unending staccato shriek of frenzy. All he could see was the broad, huge nape of the intruder moving slightly from side to side in the dark interior, stooping to complete its felon work. It kept shuffling about,—now he could see its back,—as though the narrow confines of the nesting chamber were too small for its murderous purpose.

Still Klee winnowed, frightened, angry, appalled, too taken aback to know what to do; then with sudden resolution he darted in and plucked the creature nervously on the back and was out again,—a blow as light as licking flame. Startled, the thing looked up, turned its slow face, round like a clock and blinked its enormous eyes.

It was Hoo the owl. The witch. From her ivy-curtained hole she had seen Klee carrying the rat home that morning, and observing that the eyrie was so unusually deserted had put two and two together: for she had a very large family of her own to support and her previous night's round had been very far from successful. She was a widow, too: Whittoo, her husband, had ventured out in daylight three weeks before and had had his massive forehead blown to shreds as he sat waiting for mice to run in the barnyard. Since then he had dangled upside down on a string,—the farmer's gibbet: and though each night she hooted for him there he gave no sign of answering her pleading. All Whittoo could do now was twirl and spin in the windy moonlight, a useless thing.

All Klee's nervousness vanished at the first sight of that staring face, those sunken, brooding eyes: knife-quick he switched to the attack. If she had been given time, Hoo would willingly have borne each thrust, for she was loath to forgo the rat and even now she tried again to retrieve it: but it was awkward edging out backwards with such a load, and through the thick blanketing of her plumage she could feel his lightning claws stinging again and again. It was an impossible situation; even when she tried to turn about she found herself caught fast and clicked her old bill in vexation; but at last she managed it and stood there blocking the entrance, blinking slowly.

By this time the whole tree was in an uproar, jackdaws cackling, wrens churring, sparrows chipping in, and thrushes expostulating at the top of their voices. Blackbirds came, flocking in droves from the orchard hedges, adding to the confused din: they perched in the uppermost branches, cocking their tails and jerking their heads, yelping and shouting, though whether in fear of Klee or in indignation at Hoo none knew,—they were always glad to add their voices to any hysterical chorus.

Consumed as he was with impotent fury, Klee never even noticed the commotion going on around him: all he could see was that grotesque, ungainly figure barring his entry, that lurid mask of a face. Nothing, it seemed, could disturb the owl's imperturbable calm. She went on sitting there, turning her slow face indifferently to all his attacks, as if in a stupor: then, just as Klee's exasperation was preparing a final fling, she made up her mind and went dipping heavily out across the open field, pursued by all and sundry, a crowd of execrating birds. All chased after her pell-mell, ran her to earth again in the riverside willows, where the clamour was taken up anew, though fainter now.

All except Klee. The owl had barely taken wing before he was at the entrance, anxiously looking in. None of the eyasses had been touched. They lay there as they had done that morning, and though they tried to lift their heads to him there was a spiritless air about them all: it frightened him. He emerged and stood in the entrance looking for Frikka to come, anxiety rippling in his throat.

No answer.

Turning in again he began tearing the rat open and offering it piece by piece to the young. It was their first meal that day and not a very successful one. Lack of food, even a gap of a few hours, had sapped their burning vigour : they were apathetic, droopy, until he despaired of ever tempting them, then when at last one revived all the others leaped back to life, beset him round with hungry mouths, bewildering him. The end was worse than the beginning for when the last scrap was gone not one was satisfied, only now they were all restless with discontent.

Kikikikik, he cried, looking out blankly at the vacant sky.

What could he do ? The eyasses came snuggling at his side, craving comfort, expecting him to brood them. Half-opening his wings, he allowed them to cluster inside and waited for their uncomfortable fumblings to subside, standing uneasily, his eyes still hopefully turned towards the entrance.

The undersides of the leaves and branches were gilded with bright apricot light every one ; low behind the willows the sunset was a splash of blood, a fiery face bandaged in its gauze of violet evening haze. He watched it fade, grow blurred,—an ashen smudge. His wings, unaccustomed to so unnatural a pose, were beginning to ache a little, but he did not dare to move : the querulous complaints of the young had ceased at last, and they had all settled under him for the night as best they could. He heard the first nightjars begin beyond the orchard and Hoo's mournful lament from the farmyard across the meadows . . . and then the strengthening shadows of the moon. . . . He could sense the cool moisture of dew softly settling on his constant eyes ; and prepared himself for the pale, long night. Frikka would not come now.

Day broke, blear-eyed and watery. Before dawn it had begun to rain, softly at first and then a steady downpour, hissing in the foliage and dripping from the roof tree.

Klee had to turn about and spread his wings still farther to make an awning, for although the young were partially feathered, they might easily catch cold. While it lasted he dared not leave the eyrie, and yet the eyasses were at their clamourings again, pestering him ceaselessly with sharp nudges: he wanted to get away on his day's errands,—and most of all to find Frikka.

Everything added to his worries. Somewhere, somehow, something had miscarried . . . it was all wrong, terribly wrong. If he only knew. . . .

At last a pale-eyed sun ventured a gleam or two, and the grey leaves hung quietly waiting to dry. Without even pausing to shake his soaked plumage, he set out in search of a quick breakfast, intending to be back almost immediately to tend the neglected brood. The farmyard,—that was the place: danger or no danger, he must snap up another of those ducklings and be quick about it. As he topped the elm tower he knew by the murmurous tremor of its dark leaves that it would rain again soon, and half way over the meadows he ran into a slanting shower, felt his back all stippled with pointed drops. But it was too late to turn back: his family *might* perish of exposure, but it was absolutely imperative that they should be fed, well fed—and regularly.

Approaching the farmstead, he rose to reconnoitre, scarfed in the rain-cloud—and almost immediately suffered a disappointment. The whole green space was deserted, only a red-nosed gander taking the air, trumpeting to itself. Everything else had taken cover, and though Klee slid sideways in a careful tangent, to be quite sure, there was not a sign of life round any of the coops. Not a cock crowed. Not a hen stirring. Hanging, he watched the elephantine gait of the old goose as it made its way heavily towards the drinking pool. . . .

He was just about to leave when his eye caught a movement in the grass. For a moment he did not realize the full horror of it, though he glimpsed the hard glint of steel and in a flash recalled the dangerous instrument which had sent him winging away in panic before.

It was Frikka.

She lay there wretchedly on her side, caught in those biting jaws, one wing still feebly flapping as she struggled to release her crushed body. She must have seen him hovering there, a grey shape overhead, and summoned up what tortured strength she had remaining. Now she was very still.

Klee was too confused with terror and distress to know what he was doing, what awful thing had happened. For a time he swung to and fro, calling to her to come to him, incapable of comprehending why she did not answer him, made no sign. . . . Finally he grew desperate and dived down almost on top of her, then drew up, almost fanning her face with his feverish wings. Frantically he called on her to break free, come sky-riding again—and knew that for some horrible reason she could not. He would have alighted, but the jagged fangs of the trap held him off. All he could do was winnow helplessly, calling to her all the time.

He could see her dark eye looking up at him, still clear, unstricken, but there was no meaning in its steady gaze, no recognition, neither pity nor fear. Once she beat her free wing with such iron determination that he spread his pinions expecting her to join him; but the cruel steel held firm, though even in this extremity it could not break her wild spirit. She was still the same proud Frikka . . . he could not understand why she should be grounded like this.

But now the gate banged; a great man came crunching towards them, a boy waving and whooping. In spite of his trouble Klee could not face them, and with a last frightened appeal he rose swiftly, despairing,—watched them as they stooped over her, chattering ceaselessly, incoherently, insanely.

He could see them roughhandling her, how she twisted in agony; and at the sight Klee was seared to the soul with unutterable fury. Down he tore at them, ripping the air so close to the boy's head that he had to duck, while the man bawled aloud as Klee streaked over his upraised arm.

He could do no more. All his pent feeling had been concentrated in that last sacrificial swoop: he drew off and from a safe height followed them as they carried their victim indoors. For a minute or two he hung about as though in hopes that even now she might miraculously escape, but nothing happened, and he could not stay. . . . He hurried away to his business, quartered four sides of a cornfield with smooth, mechanic flight, nipping a dormouse by the tail as it tried to dive into its hole. A joyless kill. He felt lost again, numb, glassy-eyed.

As he hurried homewards with his precious burden he observed, in passing, that the naked trap was back again in its old place in the hen-run, now a-swarm from end to end with running chicks. In the neighbouring field a man and a boy were quietly hoeing turnips, but he was too high to to regard them with anything but indifference and did not alter course one instant,—scarcely recognized them again. Still, the sight of them working together jarred his apprehension, some trouble already half-forgotten. On the crude farm fence the remains of Whittoo were dandled by the breeze, and by its side there was suspended a fresh bundle of brown drooped rags.

Nothing escaped Klee's all-seeing eye. As he hastened on, his backward glance could not fail to note the change; but merciful ignorance prevented him from recognizing its wan significance.

13

All that day and the next Klee did his best to fill a double role, fathering and mothering the whole truculent crowd,—hunter, purveyor, guardian and nurse as occasion demanded. Luckily the weather proved warm, and he was able to spend most of his time fetching and carrying, though always hard-pressed for time. At night-time he managed somehow, in a rough-and-ready sort of way—but the eyasses were very tiresome in the mornings, and he himself lacked mettle when he was a-wing, out of humour. The old fire and fury were gone, the decisive, glad mastery,—the last twist that outwitted, outdarted his quarry's fugitive leap: dully he carried on.

On the third morning it was pouring again. The young, famished after their overnight fast, were more fractious than ever, ready to fall on one another all the time on the slightest pretext. He could do nothing to pacify them. After a time he gave up trying and sat in the entrance letting the rain streak through his untidy feathers, moping. For a brief spell he was away, aimlessly whirled in the wet, wet wind, eddying overland without real purpose and butting his way back through it empty-handed after all. When he got back the eyrie was saturated and the young lay with their necks stretched out in front of them, scarcely breathing. In a dejected, makeshift fashion he tried covering them, but there was no comfort in his wet body,—it only started them striving and scuffling amongst themselves again. He could not bear to have them scrimmaging under him like that; and when in the heat of the fracas one of them nipped him in the tender part of his flank he seized it roughly, ready to tear it apart on the instant,—only he remembered himself in time and dropped it with the others.

Later in the morning he plucked up heart to fare forth again and brought back a couple of bank-voles in quick succession, which temporarily saved the situation; but how much longer could he keep it up? However earnestly he tried, his attentions were a poor substitute for what the young needed and expected: he could see that, in spite of all his efforts, all was not well with them. They were growing ever more listless, disinterested . . . he had to eat the second vole himself rather than leave it to go putrid in the nest.

Before noon the surly rain-fog rolled away, leaving the sky washed clean, a dazzling blue with the sun set in its forehead like a white-hot stone. Every freshening leaf carried its pendant of diamond and topaz lights, and as he sat drying on one of the upper branches, watching the turbid river begin to steam, he suddenly twitched his wings with new resolve. Purpose.

Off he went, crossing the orchard, aiming at the sun, leaving his territory behind in a few decisive wing-beats. Over the cornland and the dangerous wood, out into new country, an endless-stretching unfamiliar plain. A vast jig-saw of landscape, county upon county, villages smoking amid clustering trees, brook and ale-brown river threading deviously back into the heat haze, ploughland, pasture and common, far-fading to a horizon which, even to a hawk's eye, was a mystery unknown: and yet he traversed it unerringly, aiming himself at his secret goal with the sureness of a hill stream hurrying towards the hidden sea.

And in the evening, sure as fate, the curving wall of the sea came up to meet the level ridge of clouds, a frieze of ultramarine setting an edge to the endless variegation of that land of green and brown. Sped with new hope, he eased from zenith, from his highway over the frosty sky-ceiling, and came streaming earthwards in a long, effortless declivity, bursting through a gap in the low hills to survey the humped seaboard.

There, straight ahead, was his familiar marsh, the old pool winking up at him like an eye from its dark hollow, with the tawny moor climbing away to the right. For the first time for hours his flight-line was deflected,—involuntarily he veered away as he saw the lurking spinney,—but he bore straight on into the seething sea-air's crispness, overshot the land, saw the toothed skerries jutting beneath him, the sleeping tide . . . and wheeling, began to follow the line of the cliffs.

Why had he come? He did not pause to ask himself that question, any more than he thought to wonder how he had been able to find his way back to his original home without once hesitating or feeling at a loss. Yet it was only when he saw known landmarks again that he really knew where his intentions had lain: even now he did not know the reason. Some delicate sense,—something beyond purpose, hope or intelligence,—had brought him thus far; and though for a moment or two as he glided along under the darksome cliff-face he wondered vaguely what the next step was to be, the half-formed thought came and went without any twinge of doubt or misgiving. He had made a move, and the only thing to do was to follow its consequences,—let them loose themselves as easily as the unravelling of a ball of wool. They always did.

The wind had turned suddenly hostile, at cross-purposes with itself, so he avoided the boisterous headland and took a short cut overland into a broader bay where the cliffs shelved more gently to a sandy beach. Crossing over a square of beech copse (even from this height he could see the swallows, young and old, weaving and braiding around it disportingly), he heard a sad mewing and tilted his face to look up. There far above him was the lubberly Peea, her broad wings all adrift as she tried awkwardly to avoid the attentions of a gang of rooks. And here beating sombrely towards him, a smut first on the sea-line, but now a portentous figure, gaunt in sables, muttering hoarse incantations in his bearded throat as he passed,—who else but Ronka himself?

Arrived once more over the sea's edge, Klee still flew coastwise, only now his flight had taken on rather a wandering air, and from time to time he kept calling out in an aimless, feckless sort of way. A mile or so ahead a solitary oak tree stood sentinel over the tapering coastline, its roots clutching the very edge of the overtoppling basalt; and immediately above it, in the vault of the mellowing sky hung a motionless speck, a hawk. One of his own kind!

To say that Klee recalled his birthplace or that he knew his father again at such a distance would be more than the truth, but it is a fact that at the first sight of that crooked tree and the black gully yawning at its feet, he swung out to sea in a mile-long semicircle,—gave the place as wide a berth as possible. Other kestrels were living there, and that was enough,—he knew better now than to trespass in territory not his own. It was just not done.

But if this was not the place, then where?—to what end had his blind wings brought him thus far? The day was almost done, and he was far from his neglected home, a hundred miles, perhaps more, half a day's hard flying. He turned and came inshore again, a frail trifle speeding across the bay's immensity, so close to the water that the red-nebbed puffins and sooty guillemots bobbed under like corks in all directions, seeing him so close upon them. A grisly cormorant, dragon-faced, came up directly in front, took fright and lobbed itself sinuously through the next wave. Another crossed his path in full flight, cricknecked and straining,—it croaked nervously as Klee overtook and passed it easily.

The outlines of the low shore was swathed in grape-bloom mists, layer on layer, aftermath of the long summer day. Through it there peered the dark tops of trees and a blue column of smoke ascending from some village. As he came in he began calling again, this time more insistently, as though expecting to receive an answer out of the pervading stillness.

And there, sure enough, was his answer,—the generous greeting he had come so far to hear! There, soaring in the star-pointed dome, was his objective, another female!

Kee-kee-kee, he cried in shrill excitement and made up towards her eagerly. Some freedom in the way she flew,—and her very presence there at such an hour,—told him that she was unattached and that she was his for the claiming.

That old alluring cry again,—it braced him with new vigour. For a time she did not see him, and he could not understand why she was so slow to fall in and follow his luring circles, though by her vocal response he knew that she was willing. At first she seemed to stray, and there was an awkwardness marring all her motions,—a disenchantment. In a trice he saw the reason ; *his new bride was blind in her left eye!*

Keeee, he pleaded, and without further intimation or ceremony he turned and headed for the sunset hills, towards the orange afterglow. And Hirra the One-eyed followed.

Such was the beginning of Klee's new partnership ; a bargain sealed by a word unspoken. An understanding without knowledge or thought or question, yet perfect and simple from the first instant. Because his need was so desperate he sought her, and for that reason he had found her. Because he needed her she forsook all else and gave herself. He had only to call and she was ready. When he asked she came. From the start their fusion was complete : two spirits blended in a natural union.

Uncanny ? Strange ? Miraculous ?—but a bird's

everyday life is crowded with strange miracles. To cover three fields with the lofty sweep of an eye and yet spot a green lizard concealed beneath a stone; to know a shrew from a harvest-mouse or identify a beetle at a hundred feet; to plot a chartless course over half a country and return home without once wavering; to know by the shape of a cloud or a sensation in the blood what weather is brewing; to realize without thinking,—these are but avian commonplaces.

The night turned inky, no moon and only intermittent stars. The earth beneath was covered with cotton-wool, a floor of fleecy fog, a trackless level with darker islands where the higher ground (or an occasional tree) showed through: yet Klee led the way swiftly, undismayed. Before morning he had brought her to his silent eyrie, and he himself was fast asleep on his look-out branch in the elm beside the river bend.

14

NEXT morning he was out again as usual, caught three mice before sunrise and brought them to Hirra. He did not wait to watch for possible danger, but flew straight in; nor did he expect her to go through the usual ceremony (though naturally he whistled to warn her of his approach), but dropped the prey in without further ado. She spent most of the first day brooding the shivering young, nursing their strength back, coaxing them to feed, and generally accustoming herself to her new task. During his absence one of the eyasses had succumbed, but the rest soon showed every sign of recovering. She had not sense enough to remove the useless little relic, and for days it was trampled and torn underfoot until it was no longer distinguishable from the uneaten fragments which now began to accumulate in the hollow. Hirra's inexperience showed itself in more ways than one, but the brood took to their foster-mother without a murmur, and in her own rough-and-ready style she managed them well enough. She was a powerful bird and a great hand when it came to hunting, in spite of her handicap. On the second day after her arrival she followed him while he beat the bounds of their particular demesne,—the elm,—all the precise lines of demarcation,—where and where not to go. Afterwards he took her with him on an expedition, showed her the best places, his favourite corner for pigmy shrews, the wet patch where you were always sure to find a mole sooner or later. She needed no second showing. Within a week she was just as much at home in her new environment as he was and, with true feminine possessiveness, had already usurped the greater share of domestic duties. Like him, she spent most of her time foraging, but she went her own way always and never once did they meet or hail each other at a distance while out on their separate forays. When returning to the eyrie Hirra had her own procedure, too: invariably she came in over the orchard, waited in the hawthorn hedge, (a thing he would not have dreamed of doing) and then slipped home through the back entrance. Klee's trysting bough had by this time lost all its former significance. There was no sky-play nor cloud-caressing nowadays, none of the old thrills of presentation: most of the time he was hardly aware of her existence. Once when they chanced to return simultaneously he stayed behind for a moment or two, seeing her curiously moved, shuddering and arching her tail and rotating in front of him with bowed head,—but though so intense an expression of emotion could not fail to interest him, somehow it left him cold. Nothing she would do could rouse him; her presence failed to excite. . . . He had nothing to give in return for her services. Theirs was a working agreement,—no more.

All the eyasses were by this time well advanced. Usually there was at least one of them sitting at the entrance waiting for his return, sometimes three in a row, all squealing to be fed. He used to bundle them over into the hole, but there was no holding them down,—as soon as he was gone they were back again. They were very conspicuous, clambering out into the open like that, and their all but ceaseless chittering betrayed the whereabouts of the whole family to all and sundry: at first it made Klee anxious and angry, but then, as the days went by, he was himself growing ever more careless and haphazard about the whole business. It was not often nowadays that he halted in the elm before getting rid of his food-parcel, nor did he come anything like so frequently as at first. When he did, it was only the work of a moment to disentangle the prey from his talons, tear a piece off for himself and leave the carcase to be dealt with as they saw fit.

It never occurred to him to remove any of the stinking refuse with which the nest was now overloaded. Things were going well, anyway. Why trouble? Hirra was not very particular about such matters, either.

This parental indifference, however, was the ultimate cause of yet another death in the family. One afternoon he found one of the youngsters lying on its side, convulsed and staring horribly, with a solid broad pellet of undigested bone and fur wedged in its mouth. Its throat heaved uncontrollably and its breath came in great gasps, stertorously,—he could not understand what ailed it. When he returned it was no better: he stood and watched it slowly choke, how its eyes rolled up and then grew dulled, how the feathers, one by one, relaxed and turned limp at last. Very curious. . . . He could feel no regret.

Summer turned from green to gold. The cuckoo's shout was heard no more from the orchard avenues, and the voices of singing birds were stilled,—all but the monotonous, stammering reed-warblers along the river's brim. The meadows were covered now with a cloth of shining saffron,—a lake of buttercups,—Klee had to write them off as quite unworkable, though everywhere else the sweet earth was teeming with life. July, the year's lazy siesta. Drowsing at noon under his leafy panoply, he marked the clouds of brown butterflies blown sideways over the tottergrass below, paying calls at flowers as the breeze directed, or the crimson-spotted burnets skipping from stalk to stalk; he watched the shy dunnocks lead forth their second brood, creeping through the tangled hedge-bottom, thick with foxglove spires, tall fool's-parsley and riotous thistle barbs; and he yawned, fetched up a longer pellet than usual. A green woodpecker broke silence, laughing in the orchard.

In the evenings, lonesome, the slow tranquillity was broken only by the pell-mell swish of mad swifts, careering in dizzy drunken parties. A concerted scream, an electric rush of air, and they were gone, leaving the riverside strangely silent; not that he envied them their dynamic speed. All he wanted to do was sit quietly by himself and preen his worn feathers. He was feeling rather off-colour these days. Better to take things easy awhile, skulk in the greenery.

He had little affection for the young hawks, now almost ready to fly: on the contrary, he was coming to resent their continued presence in the ash tree. They were only a liability. Parasites. His visits had become gradually more and more infrequent,—when he did summon up the necessary enthusiasm to drop in, they hardly knew him, treated him like a stranger. They lay back snarling at him, or glowered at him suspiciously, ready to strike. One of them even dared to snatch at his tail as he turned his back; and all three had grown beyond recognition,—uncouth hobbledehoys, fleering and grimacing at him. He was glad to get away again.

From a distance he watched Hirra encouraging the timid trio to be bold, but when at last one of them did manage to bridge the gap and landed sprawling in the hedge, he lost interest altogether and went for a drink in the cow-pond. The very sight of them wobbling abroad,—their helpless antics in the open field,—was more than he could stand. A couple of silly flappers, hoydens, viragos,—and that useless son!—as bungling as moorhens, garrulous as jays. To hear the noise they made,—even when there were men at work scything hay in the orchard corner,—it made him sick with fear: he would rather go anywhere, do anything, than stay and watch. He had given up trying to warn them; for however agitatedly he called they did not heed,—and Hirra seemed not to understand. Tiresome rabble,—

all they thought of was their bellies, and still they showed neither aptitude nor inclination to earn their own living. A good thing when they did.

A week later he happened to run into one of the young hawks, his son, trying its wings out in the morning breeze. It came hurrying towards him, with its loose mouth and baby-talk, expecting to receive some bauble, but Klee, completely out of patience, ignored its footling cries. When it came after him, pestering him weakly, he turned on it irritably and drove it off,—and suddenly flaring into a temper, whipped after it and knocked it head over heels for its trouble. It squawled pitifully, but he left the fool to get over it as best it could.

Hirra, of course, stayed on in the territory,—and that was only to be expected,—but they held no commerce together. The ash tree was deserted; he did not even know where she roosted these days. He himself remained faithful to his old elm, though not by any means in love with it as before: already he could sense the wanderlust impatient under his skin. The young had quietly faded out of the picture, disappeared into the wide and chancy world.

Not before time, either. He was well rid of them.

15

LAUGHING, brightest September.

Days of pure crystal. Nights a-tingle with stars, when the river holt was rich with the blue incense of wood-smoke from every cottage garden. The full time of the year.

Left to himself, all his smirched feathers shed away and his autumn dress completed, there was nothing now for Klee but to grow sleek and fat. Though half inclined to make a move, his old territory still had a strong sentimental hold upon him,—he could never quite make up his mind to leave it. It was all so familiar, and in a way he had come to regard it as his personal kingdom ; besides, there was no real *need* for him to go, forsaking plenty for a foreign field. Nevertheless, though his summer corner remained the nucleus of his life, each day he roamed a little farther, north, south, east or west as the whim took him, levying his toll from the broad countryside surrounding. Each night he returned to his comfortable elm, but each morning he extended the radius of his sphere, carving out a more extensive area with carefree pinions.

In the shorn stubbles and stooked fields partridges held their portly councils or lay on their sides basking, dusting their straw-lined bodies in the powdery soil. If they saw him hovering overhead the elders would stand and stretch their throats to crow up at him, but when he dropped lower the whole stub-winged covey took fright and whirred away. Some days the cornland was crowded with turtle doves, assembling for their southward migration, gorging themselves stiff before they departed. Those that could eat no more sat lazing in the warm wood-edges, groaning and murmuring till sundown. Their monotonous music provided more than an assurance of safety while he took an afternoon nap,—it soothed his well-fed, negligent mood. Sometimes as he snoozed amid the leaves he watched the nut-brown massive-headed hawfinches stealing through the yellow hornbeams, calling each other on with furtive whisperings,—and allowed them to pass by without disclosing his presence there: or perhaps it was a party of rosy bullfinches nervously dodging in and out of the blackthorns. . . . Klee livened up and went to find another mouse for himself. That month he reaped his richest harvest.

There was only one eventful day; an experience that left him somewhat chastened. For a week beforehand he had felt the storm's pent crisis inherent in his blood, its heavy approach. There was a band of tension tight in his head, a clot on his mind from which there was no release; his nerves were taut, expectant, all his actions jerky, unsure. Long before the first rumblings began below the dark horizon he could feel the thunderous climax mounting in his veins, the hot insistence of blood against bone. He could not escape it. And then the hooded sky swelled up, waiting to burst, towered, dark as doom, and then tottered and smashed without warning. For hours the menacing lightning warred and battled overhead; thunder exploded, tearing the clouds apart, banged and blared and buffeted the defenceless tree tops; branches split and crashed all round, leaves hissed, lashed by the maniac rain. . . .

In the shelter of a black yew border, Klee huddled in the bewildered, roaring darkness, waiting for it to ease. Noise was nothing to him, yet every time the shuttering lightning twitched at him he winced as though he had been struck; but he made no attempt to move, though by this time the torrential downpour had soaked him through. He cowered, let it stream all over his dazed body, nor did he once dare to raise his head.

In the end the storm drummed itself off into the hollow distance; the last flashes glanced across the torn heavens, flickering from cloud to cloud like pebbles shearing across the surface of a sullen tarn. Still the rain came grimly down, and all around the trees stood silent, in a winter-grey light, as though scarcely daring to believe that it was all over. But gradually the great weight was lifted; the oppressive atmosphere thinned and brightened slowly. He stood up and shook the rain out of his sodden plumage. A lark rose suddenly from the stubble, a gush of aspiring song; and the whole earth was secretly drinking, slaking its long thirst. Plants, insects and animals lifted their bowed heads and came forth from their hiding places to greet the sun,—emerged into a new, invigorating world. This tumult had not been for nothing: Klee felt the air's freshness licking coolly about his neck, a new water-clearness in his eyes,—and he was glad. He had shed the dry slough of the parched dog-days.

But when he came home to roost that evening he found it necessary to seek elsewhere. His proud elm was no more than a blistered ruin, its head lopped and the torn skin flayed from its white arms,—hardly recognizable. All that remained was a seared stump. Nor from that day on did he ever meet again with Hirra on his rounds.

Wild October came, stripping the tousled landscape.

Sterner days. Now no longer could he take his pick when or wherever he pleased. Hunting had to be resumed in real earnest, and there were times when he fared far with only meagre success. Still, there was no hardship in that, and he enjoyed the clean, rigorous life. The last lingering swarms of house-martins had gone from the riverside, but Klee remained, constantly hankering after his old quarters. At nights he had taken to haunting a beech-copse, a quiet spot and he liked it tolerably well. The ginger-bread foliage, bronzed, kestrel-coloured, was still thick enough to keep out the wind; it provided excellent camouflage during the daylight, and when the sun shone each crackling leaf reddened into a medallion of pure gold. There was not much doing in the open fields, but every hedgeside was rustling with harvest mice busily preparing their winter stores of seeds and berries: so busy that often they did not look up in time to see him coming.

On the whole he managed well enough. At least his daily routine was orderly and athletic: and if the wind was keen, why so was he,—in fine trim to face it. The life for a true haggard.

Raw November.

Still he stayed, though by this time his parish was growing even more extensive and ill-defined. In far-away fashion he maintained the illusion of keeping up his summer territory, but the original significance of that little plot of ground had long since melted into thin air; nowadays there was not enough of it to support a stay-at-home thrush. Impoverishment drove him ever further afield. The scene of his labours had to be transferred to the swarded uplands,—there were still a few voles to be taken on the southern slopes,—and the wet meads down-river where the moles were still at work. This month his diet consisted chiefly of moles, and it agreed with him better than anything. He was careful not to waste a morsel,—making a kill was a long-drawn-out business nowadays, so he made the most of every meal, filling himself with the velvet fur when the hot flesh was all gone. The only parts he did not try to stomach were the creature's podgy, pink hands: he had tried them before, but their long finger-nails scraped his throat, and each time he had suffered a retching fit as a result.

Once again he had been compelled to seek fresh night-accommodation. The beechen gold had blown away; the trees were bald. Now that its roof and walls were gone there was no shelter in the empty copse, not one warm nook in the rime-white branches. Instead, he cradled himself in the depths of a fir plantation.

December came and still he did not feel the pinch. The flaxen stubbles were exchanged for new-broken ploughland, —and Klee was not above following the puling gulls in the hope of worms, or perchance a dozy mouse uprooted from its nest underground. The fields were strewn with bird-flocks,—gluttonous woodpigeons, rooks and jackdaws in their sober armies,—from aloft they looked like ink-spots sprayed on the faded land. From any height he could tell the crested lapwings by their own peculiar mannerism,—tripping along and then up-ending stiffly to gobble grub or leather-jacket. Then there were the starlings, multitudes, armies of them, probing the earth,—pushing crowds, —squabbling, jumping like fleas. And countless others concealed in the wet grass everywhere,—finches, larks and buntings, gay-winged, ready to start up at any moment and go prancing off in sprightly, merry bands. Happy-go-lucky troupers. Picaresques.

Glaucous skies and a brassy sun. Yet some days, screened by the firs, he could laze an hour away in its faint warmth, watching the redwings filch the luscious berries from his yew tree.

Gluk, gluk! they cried, knowing he was there, but never ceasing to guzzle for a moment. Sometimes when he was at a loose end he would play dog-in-the-manger,—squat down on the old yew's topmost spray and listen to their nervous protests as they tried,—diffidently,—to sneak back. He had even sampled the fleshy, scarlet fruit. It had a bitter, tonic flavour, not entirely displeasing.

So it went on, an uneventful cavalcade of days. An aimless, airy existence. All thoughts of making a real move had left him now. Without really considering his own case he was content, self-satisfied. There was nothing that he really lacked,—or, if he wanted it, that he could not easily find. His daily routine was as regular as clockwork. Every hour had its appointed haunt, its appropriate activity. Each morning he was sure, for instance, to start the same three snipe speeding up from the far corner of the marsh and meet with the same gulls on their way to the distant city's garbage dumps. Each afternoon the same goldfinches clustered upon the row of dead teasels which lined the sunny side of the copse; they always rose in a body as he passed over, but settled again at once, tweezering out the last of the dust-dry seeds with their spindle bills. And when he came to roost, there, sure enough was Skretch the barn owl, sitting on his post waiting for the twilight to thicken. An unfailing regularity ordered their way of life as well as his.

The dead embers of the year. Cold ashes, silver-grey.

When the frosts came, Klee's time-table had to be revised once more. For a week he subsisted on next to nothing—and still the earth was iron-bound, shrivelled with ice. There was a greyness over the whole flinty land, an immense brooding silence. Try where he might—and he tried everywhere—the fields were empty, every hedgerow deserted. Through the murky daylight and endless nights not a whisper was to be heard in the black woods, only the occasional splitting of a branch as the ice exerted its bitter stranglehold. The grass was prickly underfoot with it, every blade steely and stiff. Branches were brittle, sheathed in glass, awkward for perching.

The cold he could endure; most of the time, indeed, he was scarcely aware of its penetrating shrewdness. But lack of food was a misfortune against which he could not fight. It sapped all his keen spirit. Before he knew it, all his reserve of strength was gone: he relapsed into an almost comatose condition,—sat half the day in a bare treetop with his head hunched between his numbed shoulders, the very picture of abandoned misery. He felt no hunger pang, no pain, no pity for himself, no fear, but he was tired, listless, droopy. The only thing to do was to shut himself up within himself and wait. . . .

Gradually he sank deeper into this state of wintry reverie, a blur of dreariness, only to revive with a start, wakened by some movement close at hand. Once he tried dropping on a bunch of sparrows scuffling under a hay-stack,—desperate resolve,—but they were too agile for him, and after the initial effort he had neither interest nor energy to pursue them.

On the eighth morning what senses he had left remaining were aware of a mystifying change,—even Klee's eye was dazzled by its brilliance. He was used to revelling in ethereal radiance, but now the whole earth was white, the low sky lead-heavy, dark. At first it bewildered him. He shook the freezing coronet of snow from his head and set out to find his bearings in an unfamilar landscape.

It was hopeless. Everywhere he went was blanketed over, every ditch choked with whiteness; and, as he breasted the upland slopes, he ran head-on into the whirling storm of snowflakes. He battled on, blinded by the racing blizzard, trying in vain to examine the muzzy surface beneath him for the first hint of a movement: but its rage was too much for him,—it carried him sideways, lost in the arctic murk. Even now he refused to give up. When the scudding flakes had thinned a little he peered through the swivelling drifts, looking for the breathing-holes of some buried animal, but saw none, only a solitary blackbird trying in vain to dig its way through to the dark leaf-mould.

Some uncommon sense carried him to the milder coast again, but this time he had arrived too late: the whole shore was covered with the same white layer to the very edge of the waves. A gun-metal sky and a gale that had flung the surf in his face a mile and more before he saw the first breakers forbade all thoughts of crossing. He had scarcely will enough to struggle back from the wind-picked beach (white, stark as a bone) to the low fields behind the sea-wall. He could go no farther. This was the end.

By this time it was already almost dark and still the deadly flakes came skirling and thickening. He flew low, close to the embankment, looking for some place of shelter; and suddenly, wonder of wonders! he spotted a smear of black in the otherwise unspotted expanse—fresh soil scattered on the side of a mole's winter fortress. Some creature was digging there. He could see its arched rump heaving as it scraped the earth out behind it . . . and without thinking he fell upon it.

At any other time Klee would have been more circumspect. Famine had made him rash. The moment he saw it, he knew it was no mole,—no mole would stir from its fastness in such weather,—but in that very moment he had fixed his talons firmly in the creature's back.

But if Klee was desperate so too was the weasel! All day it had been trying to track down hedgehog hibernating or embedded mole, winding through the underground mazes of tunnels and galleries without success, until at last it was crazy for blood. It had just begun to dig a new entrance,—unearth the brute somehow,—when a stinging pain in the small of its back made it twist round.

Klee's first blow had miscalculated. The little beast was as long and lithe as an eel: instead of piercing its vitals he had merely fastened on its haunches. In a flash it slewed round nimbly and darted at his head. He felt the hot stench of its breath in his eyes, the fangs at his throat,—and bared his bill at it with equal savagery. The weasel was not much bigger than a mole,—in actual bulk a good deal smaller,—but it was possessed of a concentrated vigour which was quite startling. It did not wait to recover from its initial reverse: it fought back with such implacable fanaticism that Klee took fright and would have flown up, if only he could have got his claws free in time. Too late, —and in that instant he knew he had met his master . . . his adversary had wreathed him over and got him by the fleshy part of his wing. Its paws pinned him, it bit again and again with its sharp, venomous jaws. Another moment and it would have had him down, but he wrenched sideways and managed to hold it off, flaying its hind parts uselessly with its free wing. Now they lay on their sides face to face, the reek of its fur in his nostrils, heaving and pounding, spattered with earth and snow. He could see its bloodshot, fanatical eyes, its close-cropped ears that lay back on its flat head, the blunt snout snuffling not an inch away ; and drove the hook of his bill into it before it could snake at him again. The weasel snarled, recoiled. Before it knew what was happening the tables were turned. Without giving it time to regain control Klee had shifted his lacerating foothold and bestridden it. His talons clenched in its ermine stomacher ; with his wings he flogged its bleeding flanks. Then with his last strength he lifted it bodily up and struggled into the fighting air. Once, twice, that fatal load was too much for him : the pair of them sank back into the scattering softness. Once it seized him by the other wing,—he heard its teeth gritting into the bone,—but he tore loose and was off again, flayling the air. He would *not* let go. His mouth was gaping, his heart bursting, but he headed into the blizzard and forced himself to rise. He had to bend double all the time to ward off those slavering jaws, for even in this fix his enemy was by no means done for. It wriggled, tangled its torn limbs round his trailing legs, and shrieked to free itself.

Ten feet, fifteen, twenty feet,—that was as high as he could get, lugging his dangerous burden towards the sea-wall.

Without warning, a great figure loomed out of the

curdled atmosphere, an ogre shape. A man! The sudden apparition of a human being as close as that riveted all Klee's attention; he looked up,—tried to swerve,—and in that distracted instant the weasel had him by the throat. He was helpless, choking. Blood spouted in his eyes. He crumpled, tumbled in a broken heap into the smothering snow.

The next moment was a weltering nightmare, hot fear and pain. He could still feel the murderous clinch of his assailant, greedily sucking his life-blood away; and could do nothing. But as he lay on his back, awaiting the death blow, the weasel suddenly left off, chattered angrily with upturned head; and before it could spring sideways a great blow had knocked it flying.

Klee froze with terror, seeing the monstrous stature of a man standing over him. He lay back, rigid, paralysed with the very intensity of his wild aversion, eyes staring, feet ready to clutch. . . . And then the ultimate horror,—he almost swooned,—a huge leathery hand folded about his thin body and thrust him roughly into the musty darkness.

16

DRY spleen was eating his heart away.

The wooden shack in which they had shut him was narrow and dark, with a little square of light high up in one of its cobwebbed walls, beyond his straining: a noisome prison. Everything about that evil-smelling interior filled him with resentment and bitter loathing: all day he sat on the handle of a wheel-barrow with his head in a corner, brooding over his unspeakable hatred. Imprisonment could not blunt the razor-edge of his wild spirit nor dull its smouldering heat: as he grew stronger again it would have burst out in a leaping spark of flame, only it could not,—he was too cabined, cribbed, confined. Baffled, his soaring energies could find no outlet,—they turned inwards upon him and made him sour, insidious. Sometimes he was seized with strange fits and dashed himself again and again at the bare walls until he sprawled exhausted and nigh senseless; but most of the time he just sat there, nursing his grievance in silence. A recluse, tantrum-twitched.

Slowly but surely this unnatural new life was making a monomaniac of him, oppressing him with its dark tedium. Each day the place grew more and more like a mad-house.

But if it was bad now it had been far worse at first, almost unbearable. In the early days of his captivity he was too weak to feed himself, or even to want to feed, unable to stand on his feet. They had seized him in their bruising hands, pinning his wings and turning him on his back to prise open his clenched mandibles and force strange meats down his unwilling throat. Never in his life had he experienced such an excruciating intensity of fear as then.

To be held in a vice, or even to be touched,—it drove him crazy, and yet there was no escape, nothing he could do but cower, stiff and staring with terror. His eyes dilated, his body shrank, his very soul constricted to a tight wedge of horror, whenever he saw that enormous hand outstretched to take him. If he could, he would have died, but they forced him to live. They washed his wounds, probed them with metal instruments, hooded his shriekless eyes while they rubbed his soreness with acid liquids that aggravated it like fire. There was a hot light, a host of objects that glittered unsteadily around him, red faces and strident voices; worst of all, no sky,—only a garish pattern of colours on the low ceiling. Then when at last their devilry was done he was taken out from the smoky room and deposited in the dark shed. There he was left to himself to recover as best he could.

Nothing they could do could tempt him to unbend. The intense aversion blazing in his eyes,—the inflexible ferocity of his aloofness commanded respect: and even in the depths of his own fear he knew by their clumsy fingers that they were nervous, unsure how to approach him. Sometimes they dropped him hastily, like a hot cinder.

Most of the time, however, he was left to himself,—but not in peace. Even when the door slammed and the crunch of their heavy boots had died away he would still lie there, rigid, his whole frame locked in a stony fixity of apprehension. It might be a quarter of an hour before he allowed himself to relax: then he dared to let his real self, what was left of it, reassert itself,—slowly, cautiously, like a hurt snail feeling its way out from its shell again. They had at last given up waiting for him to eat and drink while they were there. One thing above all else he could not endure,—to be watched. No matter how tempting the bait, he would rather starve than touch it in their presence. They had tried him with mice and sparrows, with a fresh rat neatly dissected, pushing it between his talons to let him feel it, but all to no avail; he turned mulish, wooden, rolled over and lay back stiffly like a dead thing.

Finding that they could do nothing with him they next tried subterfuge. They used to take him into the house and leave him by himself in an empty room; but he could hear the excited whisperings of the children, and more than once he glimpsed the high-lights of their eyes spying at him behind the crack in the door; and Klee continued stubbornly immobile. So long he lay, in fact, that they thought he was shamming death, but it was not that,—at the very sight of human form all his nerves seized up in an instant; his brain went blank, taut, snapped shut like a steel trap. They had tried this on him time and time again without result, and then one day, impatient at the delay, two of the children opened the door and rushed in, trying to catch him. That was too much . . . he shot up between their waving arms, sent a vase crashing from the mantelpiece and almost broke his neck against the invisible wall of light.

After that they did not take him indoors again. Each morning they opened the shed-door,—a dreadful, jarring sound,—flung a handful of meat on the floor and spent a minute or so changing his water. As soon as he heard them coming he went scurrying into the darkest corner or hid himself behind the woodpile. If he had dared he would have made a dash for it, for the bright aperture filled him with sudden aspiration, but he was completely unnerved by the shambling figure of his gigantic gaoler. That awful presence did more than his own physical weakness to disable him. He dared not take his eyes away. . . .

But the moment the door was banged to again, his wild hope blazed again and he flung himself up at the windows, tapping at the smudged glass, trying to gain a foothold, tumbling back at last when the effort proved too much for him. In half-hearted fashion he fell to examining the provisions they had left him, turned them over dejectedly and swallowed a piece. It was not bad, but however viciously he tore it, it was tame work at mealtimes. He craved the excitement of a full-blooded kill. And there was no trusting these captors of his: there were times when the door shut and the footsteps did *not* die away. They remained behind, peering in at him. He could see their shadows blocking the sunlight, feel the dull weight of their bodies pressing in against the wood,—and no matter how quiet they were in their efforts to deceive him, there was no concealing the slow rhythm of their breathing. He could never trust them in anything. He lay still and waited for them to go.

That was his whole life, a tremulous watching and waiting with morbid intervals, dozing and dreaming. Suspicion,—Fear,—Hate,—but most of the time just a dulled state of stupidity shot through with occasional spasms of rebellious hope.

To while away the tedium,—and for the sake of exercise,—he used to walk up and down the rough wainscot, follow its perimeter right round, nosing inquisitively every inch of the way, poking his head into draughts as if almost expecting to find some hidden exit. Round and round he hobbled, incapable of realizing the futility of his blind efforts. What else was there to do? After a week or two he gave it up and just sat.

At last there came a time when he grew almost resigned to his strange isolation; after all, there had always been a lazy streak in his nature, and provided he was well fed he enjoyed more than anything to spend a languid hour at his ease. In a way, this pampered, cloistral life suited him well enough. Now that they left him so severely alone he had begun to interest himself in his new appearance again, nibbling and smoothing his lustrous feathers, rinsing them in his drinking-bowl and then preening again until he was immaculate. His wounds had healed without a scar, and thanks to the care which he bestowed upon himself during his long convalescence his rehabilitation was, to the outward view, complete, perfect. Oh, yes, there were times when he felt quite pleased with himself. In certain lights the window shone like a mirror,—he could see his own tarnished reflection peering in at him from the outside world and used to work himself up into a flutter of excitement as he clung to the narrow sill, trying to make it understand that he was there. At the sight of that dim hawk face his throat burst out into vehement, mad lyrics; he tapped at the glass, ran his head against it,—anything to declare his presence there. Abortive longing. His frantic efforts could achieve no contact. His shadow-fellowship brought no satisfaction. Every time his hopes were dashed bodily to the ground, and to comfort himself he had to start preening all over again.

How long it had been going on like this he did not know,—several weeks, probably. Some days the interior was quite stifling, and by the sound of hidden bird-calls, —sprightly sparrows on the roof or sonorous procession of rooks overhead,—he knew that the Spring was at hand. He knew it, too, by the gentler sway of the wind in the rafters,—and even the obscurity of the shack received something of the sun's cleaner radiance. When it shone through each afternoon he had to quit his perch on the wheelbarrow, for the window acted like a burning-glass, —the spot-light shaft was too hot to be comfortable.

Not that he needed such external reminders. He could feel the season's change simmering in his blood, the old passion returning, new lust for action. To have to sit about like this, useless, forgotten, when the winds of

March were calling! It was driving him insane. One of these days he would dash his brains out against that mocking glass.

One morning he was sitting in his usual position when the door was thrust open,—a scurry of leaves,—and hastily shut again. He cringed, expecting the man to appear, but when the footsteps had died away again he was aware of a hunchback figure standing there in the semi-darkness just inside the entrance. It was a grey common gull, blood dripping from its shattered wing, far gone by the look of things. It made no effort to move but remained where it had been dropped, in a dazed stupor, its eyes half closed. Gradually, as though its legs were melting away for weariness, it sank into a sitting posture.

Klee shifted round and eyed the new inmate with interest. It had not seen him, perched there on the wheelbarrow; indeed it is doubtful whether the eye of this latest casualty would have registered anything if it had had the energy left to look up. Its yellow beak drooped still lower on its pouted breast. . . .

Kikikikik!

The gull did not move an eyelid.

Kikikik! Klee called peremptorily.

It remained stolid, apathetic. Somehow, its wretchedness irritated him, the mere fact of its presence there was enough to bring out the devil in him. He jigged up and down on his perch, beside himself, torn by conflicting impulses, chattering all the time in a pæan of uncontrollable hysteria. The cancerous hate that had grown so long, so secretly, inside him came suddenly to a head,—burst in a blinding riot of action. He flopped down and seized the gull by the small of the back. Its plumage was thick and padded but he felt his talons strike home. It squirmed a little and turned its head to look at him with its patient sad eyes, but it made no offer to struggle, no protest.

Klee's mad crying quickened, rose to crescendo, one unending shriek. A murderous rage detonated inside him: for a moment he was transformed into a leaping maniac, a firework of agonized fury. He drove his talons deeper into the creature's soft neck.

In the midst of this noisy scuffle the door was suddenly flung open and he was pushed violently aside. The man snatched up the limp figure of the gull, roared out and would have struck him; but he dodged between his slow legs, scampered along the floor in a panic, and, before he had time to realize what he had done, he was out. Out in the bright daylight! He blinked, unable to understand how he had got there, but the man shouted again, louder; a boy came running at him, flourishing a stick. For a moment his terror made him hesitate, then he darted sideways and rose into the wind. Some missile came whirring after him, almost grazing his tail, causing him to stagger in his flight,—but on and up he bored, away from the raucous cries, the angry voices. As he cleared the rooftop the sea-wind caught him; for a second he yawed unsteadily, lurched drunkenly,—as a sick man will do the first time he leaves his bed and tries his dithering legs.

But Klee was not sick. Not now. There, patterned below him, were green fields again and the wrinkled ploughland, the endless shore and the curled shape of gracious hills peering over the world's blue edge. And far above,—his immediate objective,—was the bright clear zenith, serried with clouds. He was free,—free! Never again would he need his freedom so much as now,—now!—nor taste it with such joy. Free! Now that it had no power to jostle him or knock his wings awry he surrendered himself utterly to the wild wind,—he was sure of himself again. With every beat he felt his old mastery returning, and raced on into the heavens, the air singing and frothing between his crisp keen feathers.

Up he drove, straight for the sun's white circle, growing ever smaller as he left the earth behind him,—thrush-size, wren-size, beetle-size,

a bead, a

speck

fading,—

until at last he merged and dwindled away for ever

into the infinite azure

of his native

sky